# THE RESEARCH ADVENTURE

Barbara Lebock

Consulting Editor:
**PETER I. ROSE**
*Smith College*

# MYRON GLAZER

Smith College

# THE RESEARCH ADVENTURE

## promise and problems of field work

WITH A FOREWORD BY PETER I. ROSE

Random House  New York

Library of Congress Cataloging in Publication Data

Glazer Myron.
The research adventure.

Bibliography: p.
1. Social Sciences—Field work. 2. Social sciences—Methodology. I. Title. II. Title: Promise and problems of field work.
H61.G554    300′.7′2    71-38985
ISBN 0-394-31709-2

Manufactured in the United States of America.

Typography by Jack Ribik

**468  975**

FOR OUR PARENTS
**IDA AND NATHAN GLASSER**
AND
**REBECCA AND BEN MIGDAL**
WITH WARMEST
AFFECTION

# a note on sources
# and a word of appreciation

Much of the material for the first draft of this volume was garnered from available books and journals. The draft was then sent to all those field workers whose experiences had been cited. They most generously responded with critical comments and provided further insights that I incorporated into subsequent revisions. Thus, while I have quoted very little from published sources, I have included statements from the many letters, telephone calls, and personal conversations that I had with these researchers. The willingness of the field workers to answer many sensitive questions merits my deep gratitude and warm personal thanks.

# FOREWORD

Several years ago, while planning a new format for our introductory course in sociology, we decided to introduce a series of lectures on "The Research Process." The idea was to give incoming students some sense of what sociologists do when "in the field," what they look for and how they go about it. By way of introduction I was to give four or five lectures on the history of sociology, with particular emphasis on empirical research and on various methods of sociological inquiry. My colleague, Mickey Glazer, was to follow with several weeks of discussions dealing with the problems one faced when actually undertaking a research project.

My lectures included discussions of Auguste Comte's ideas about a study of society in which the theoretical, empirical, and practical could be combined; an introduction to the legacy of Marx and Weber and Durkheim; and a quick survey of American sociology—beginning with Ward and Sumner and the debates over involvement and detachment; Robert Park, the "Chicago School," and the blossoming of the "natural history" approach; Parsons and the functionalists; the surveys of the 1940s; Riesman and Mills and others in the 1950s; and the challenge of the "New Sociology" in the 1960s. To illustrate the variety of research techniques (from *verstehen* to the sample survey), and the relation of theory to research, certain representative studies were briefly introduced.

It was interesting (so the students said) and useful, too. These responses pleased us, especially since we hoped that those who were to become sociology majors would have already begun to know who was who and would be stimulated to start study-ing the "classics" early in their careers. But to me at least, it was pretty standard fare.

Glazer's lectures followed, and as I listened I realized that while my approach may have been somewhat innovative, he was touching on many issues that few graduate students, let alone neophytes, ever considered seriously. And he was offering his views on the core methodological problems and ethical issues in a clear, concise, and convincing fashion, a fashion that even beginners could comprehend.

His presentations picked up where mine left off. He went beyond the encapsulated history of sociology, beyond my com-mentaries on technique, beyond what the students had read (and we all had discussed) in Merton's famous piece on research and theory. He began in a highly personal way, discussing his own experiences in conducting a study of the professional and political attitudes of Chilean university students several years before, mapping out the project like a film scenario, and setting the stage through a series of flashbacks.

I was especially impressed with his second lecture in which he compared what he and his wife had been doing and feeling in Chile with what others had experienced in the field, including some of those I had mentioned in my lectures (such as William Foote Whyte, author of *Street Corner Society*, Gerald D. Berre-man, who wrote *Hindus of the Himalayas* and *Behind Many Masks*, and Herbert J. Gans, author of *The Urban Villagers* and *The Levittowners*).

Glazer's last lectures dealt with the ethics of social research and included some reference to what the investigator owes to his subjects, to his colleagues, and to his sponsors. While the students seemed most interested in the first two recipient groups, those of us on the staff were intrigued by the issues raised about the last, since the infamous episode of "Project Camelot" was still very much on our minds (and particularly on Glazer's, for he had been in Chile shortly before the story of the sociological study sponsored by the United States Army broke, and was subsequently accused of being a CIA plant).

Some weeks after the course was over (and many discussions later), I suggested to Glazer that he consider writing up his lectures in a more systematic form with an eye toward publication, perhaps as a volume for undergraduates on "The Promise and the Problems of Field Research." He was interested; so was Random House. *The Research Adventure* is the result.

In many ways this book is unique; not so much in the subject matter but in the approach to it. Here Glazer takes the reader through the stages of the field research process: deciding on the project and the method; considering the problem of gaining acceptance and establishing a legitimate identity (while facing the ever-present suspicions of those studied); learning one's way around; getting behind the scenes or, as Erving Goffman puts it, "backstage"; dealing with data; and, finally, considering the matter of what knowledge for whom. Moreover, Glazer introduces the reader to a number of well-known (and several lesser-known but equally important) studies and their authors: Whyte and Berreman, Elliot Liebow and Gans, Pierre L. van den Berghe and his work in South Africa, Arlene Kaplan Daniels' research on the military, Laud Humphreys' studies of impersonal sex, Project Camelot and its critics, and many others.

Every author whose work is discussed in detail was given the opportunity to review Glazer's treatment of his or her material. Most responded with advice and encouragement. Many were critical of certain interpretations. Some caught the author in an error of fact or judgment. Some felt more (or less) should be said about a particular incident or episode. Each comment and criticism was carefully weighed in the revisions of the original manuscript.

There was unanimity, too; unanimity in the desire of all to have the book published—and quickly.

My initial enthusiasm for the project seemed to be clearly warranted. Now, with Mickey Glazer, I hope that students will find this an exciting and provocative volume, and that the controversial ideas presented here will stimulate them to undertake research adventures of their own.

                                              PETER I. ROSE

*South Wellfleet, Massachusetts*

# PREFACE

My original purpose in writing *The Research Adventure* was to introduce students to its challenges and excitement. As I studied it, spoke to and corresponded with its participants, I became increasingly aware of its complexities and ever more concerned about the problematic nature of research relationships. I am far more troubled now than I was three years ago. Yet, I am also more secure in the knowledge that a close analysis of social science field work is a rewarding and enriching endeavor.

I have been fortunate in coming to know many of the people whose work I had read earlier. Together we have pondered over the most challenging ethical issues. Many other old friends and recent acquaintances have also probed their own thoughts in the most forthright manner while challenging my assertions. In essence, the last few years have been precious ones for me and I proudly identify those who have been an integral part of it.

All of the researchers who are cited in the text read the manuscript in its various versions and contributed to the development of the book in a vital way. Arlene Kaplan Daniels and Jerry Hyman, particularly, did a line by line critique. I benefited from their no-holds-barred observations.

Old and dear friends provided insightful criticism and forced me to look more courageously at my initial conclusions. Burt Goodman, Terry and Fay Lichtash, Joel Migdal, Art Liebman, Howard Boughey, Phil Green, Michael Irwin, Charles Sackrey, Dennis Hudson, Dave Leverenz, Irving Louis Horowitz, Joel Arem, Randy Huntsberry, Bill Shepherd, and David Schimmel, Bob Cook, and Ely Chinoy were among my most persistent critics.

Colleagues and comrades who were well acquainted with my Chilean research added their own expertise. Ben Burnett, John Shearer, Aury Fernandez, and Frank Bonilla once again generously contributed, as did Marcello Truzzi, William Domhoff, Norman Denzin, Herbert Gans, Michael Useem, Bob Bohlke, and Murray Gruber, all of whose own work broadened my interpretations. Wilbert E. Moore has deeply influenced both my work in comparative sociology and my writing style.

Peter I. Rose, editor, colleague, and close friend, stimulated and prodded me to pursue the truly important issues. I hope he knows what a central part he has played in the completion of this effort.

Penina Migdal Glazer, my co-worker on the Chilean project, has been a constant and cherished companion in my subsequent research. She has read every page of this book more times than I care to admit. In addition, her own historical investigation of the American radical movement has served as a continued reminder of the still unresolved major social problems that have long plagued this nation.

There are several others whose contribution has been central. Agnes Shannon, secretary to the social science departments at Smith College, merits the great respect and appreciation of all of us who have become so dependent on her efficient and cheerful manner. She has helped make my years at Smith most pleasant ones indeed. Norma Lepine has typed and retyped every page of the manuscript. I doubt that others are ever sufficiently aware just how crucial are the understanding and encouragement of a good secretary. Thank you, Mrs. Lepine, for all your efforts.

Frank Zabawa and his staff, particularly Leona Superba, spent many hours reproducing the manuscript. I could not have gathered the reactions of so many readers without this essential assistance. Barbara Cook, Julia Markrich and Ann Thompson deserve recognition for their assistance during various stages of this project.

Finally, I dedicate this book to our parents. Their lives and struggles on behalf of their children and others have won our love and profound respect. Bubi and Pa, Riv and Ben, you are close to our hearts.

MICKEY GLAZER

# CONTENTS

## PART B. SUSPICION INTENSIFIED

Wherein field workers defined as dangerous outsiders seek ways to break through the barriers by distinguishing themselves from hostile forces and by attempting to meet the needs of local people. Alterations in the researcher's bearing and attitudes are also made. Project Camelot is rejected and provides a lesson in the pitfalls of sponsorship. Charges of intrigue and intervention plague many investigators. The increasing role of the United States military and the C.I.A. in overseas research has exposed social scientists to wrath, suspicion, and condemnation. Cases discussed include:

## CHAPTER II
## PART A. LEARNING ONE'S WAY AROUND

Wherein initial acceptance is shown to be only a first hurdle. The challenges of overinvolvement, bias, and response to social injustice confront many field workers. The researcher must decide whether to segregate his role as collector of reliable data from his desire to criticize publicly, or to be an immediate agent of social change. Role conflict, the author argues, is an integral part of the researcher's life style. His socialization must emphasize the ability to live with uncertainty and ambiguity. The sustenance of others is crucial. Local families, co-workers, wives or husbands and children provide essential support during periods of frustration and self-doubt. Cases studied include:

## PART B. REACTING TO SOCIAL INJUSTICE

Wherein field workers confront the ugly specter of massive suffering. Those studying other nations decide to pursue their research and ward off feelings of guilt and impotence by declaring their research as eventual weapons in the struggle for human dignity. Colleagues working within their own nation occasionally assume the activist role and expose themselves to immediate and severe retaliation. Cases studied include:

## CHAPTER III
### PART A. PEERING BEHIND THE STAGE

Wherein the essence of the research endeavor is analyzed. The social scientist, of necessity, attempts to penetrate into the shadowy areas of social life. Rackets, sexual outlets, social inequality, all come under scrutiny. The debunking motif is shown to be crucial. The tension between researchers and respondents becomes ever clearer. The field worker's techniques of probing are matched against the subjects' facility to camouflage sensitive areas. Cases studied include:

### PART B. RESISTANCE INTENSIFIED

Wherein it is shown that resistance is not without effect. Researchers are condemned as spies, subversives, traitors, and busybodies by respondents, government officials, and the researcher's own colleagues. All researchers, the author maintains, must clearly understand the values inherent in their own efforts and weigh them against the needs of those they desire to study. Cases studied include:

## CHAPTER IV
### PART A. THE DIMENSIONS OF RECIPROCITY

Wherein the respondents may ask for a return on their investment of time, effort, and faith. The rewards of research too often seem to fall to the researcher. Others seldom benefit directly. There are often unforeseen consequences from assisting the investigator. Individual weakness may be exposed. Group life can be held up to public ridicule. Information may be made available to powerful and hostile interests. Field workers agonize over what loyalty they owe and to whom. The inherent conflict between probing and yet safeguarding the rights of respondents is shown to be almost insoluble. Cases studied include:

Wherein field workers reevaluate the gains and costs of probing into the life styles of the poor and powerless. Some researchers call for greater commitment to providing direct services to these people. Radical sociologists demand more study of elite groups. Let their lives be an open book, they urge. It is apparent, the author observes, that the more powerful sectors of any society can shield themselves from the scrutiny of social scientists and can encourage the direction of research. The social scientist must strive to maintain his independence from administrative organizations. Intense self-awareness and critical analysis of commitments are crucial in this endeavor. Constant debunking of their own work styles is crucial if social scientists are to meet their increasing responsibilities. Issues discussed include:

# THE RESEARCH ADVENTURE

# INTRODUCTION

The walk from the bus stop to the University of Chile was a long one. With the brilliant May sun as a companion, I strolled through the quiet middle-class neighborhood. The houses, small stores, and open windows through which I could see maids beating rugs and waxing floors had long since become familiar sights.

I reached the busy intersection, watched the crowded buses roar by, and, respecting the reckless Santiago drivers, carefully made my way to the University side of the street. The low, dull green wall that enclosed the campus presented a panorama of Chilean political life. The youth branches of all the political parties had inscribed their slogans in paint, and a small revolutionary group denounced them all as it proclaimed its own position.

The stone barrier gave way to the gates to the campus, and I passed the students scurrying to class, to the cafeteria, or to jobs in the city's distant center. My first stop was the School of History.

No matter how trying or difficult the day before had been, I faced each morning deeply excited about my research and life in Santiago. Given an abundance of financial resources, unlimited time, and all the other paraphernalia provided by an accommodating genie, I knew that I would choose to do exactly what I was doing and would elect to be exactly where I was.

A year earlier, in preparing for our Chilean research, my wife, Penina, and I had spent a summer in Mexico practicing Spanish, had traveled widely there and, later, in Peru, and had enjoyed the beauty and complexity of Indian cultures. Our explorations had continued in European-oriented Argentina and Uruguay. During our first six months in Chile, we had ventured to most sections of the capital city and had marveled at the beauty of the lakes and the snow-capped mountains of the nation's south.

The contrasts in natural beauty and cultural richness, on the one hand, and man-inspired suffering, on the other, had engraved themselves deeply in our thoughts. We could not come to grips with the Chilean beggar children, the pathetic tarpaper homes, and the dreams of revolutions unfulfilled. The sense of United States complicity haunted us even as we learned at first hand just how well so many Latin Americans lived at their countrymen's expense.

We had met student leaders from all the major Chilean political groups and had interviewed several hundred of their peers about their professional goals and political commitments. We were fascinated by the emotional intensity of the hard-fought national presidential campaign. As I approached a group of familiar faces near the student cafeteria, there was no doubt that these months had been and would continue to be one of the high points of my life.

Yet before this day was over I learned that many previously friendly students had begun to question my motives and the objectives of the study. They accused Penina and me of being foreign spies, intent on exposing radical students to the C.I.A. I became deeply defensive about the legitimacy of my efforts while recognizing full well that our accusers had grave reasons to be suspicious of my country and its citizens. In a few short days I had to defend my work not only to others but also, more importantly, to myself. I had to confront many painful questions similar to those that honest field workers have raised, if only in private, for generations: Should Penina and I have been gathering data on the political views of Chilean students? Had I gained the active cooperation of student leaders by promising far more than I could ever deliver? Indeed, couldn't my material eventually be used against the very people I promised to help? Were social scientists ultimately the manipulators of the oppressed and actually in the service of the powerful?

As I faced these questions I gained a deeper appreciation of the nature of the research adventure. I learned that it entailed far more than traveling to distant lands. More significantly, it meant that the honest field worker must constantly examine his own motivations and goals.

These feelings of exhilaration, suspicion, and self-doubt have been shared by countless other social scientists in a thousand different settings. In this volume I attempt to capture some of their reactions. Many of the events retold are part of social science folklore. Generations of students have read and absorbed some of this material. Most other experiences related here are far more obscure or recent. In either instance, the message is the same. The satisfactions, excitement, frustrations, challenges, and agonies of field research are not time bound. They are as real and relevant today as when they occurred—last year, a decade ago, or during the last century.

The questions posed by field work continue to be fundamental for seasoned and neophyte researchers as well as for others concerned with the many varieties of human experience:

How does the social scientist identify himself and his project in an unfamiliar environment?

What are the various reactions of local people to the arrival of the "stranger"?

How can the social scientist observe beyond the walls and masks of group life?

Are there taboo areas into which he dare not probe?

Under what conditions will the researcher be accused of exploiting respondents and informants?

What responsibility does the social scientist have to help those he has studied?

The questions are crucial and must be constantly expressed, discussed, and evaluated. Those who would participate in the adventures of research must continually confront the most challenging questions of scientific ethics and social responsibility. For we are deeply "involved in mankind."

In the process of exploring these and other related issues, I will highlight four problems facing social scientists in a variety of field work settings. These problems, which comprise the chapter headings in this volume, emphasize the challenges associated with four major stages of the research process:

1. gaining the *acceptance* of local informants and respondents;
2. adapting to the special demands of the research setting, particularly avoiding *overidentification* with respondents, the tendency toward *biased* observations, and the *debilitating* impact of social injustice;
3. collecting material about *sensitive* issues of social life and resolving the ethical issues inherent in the often competing value systems of the researchers and the respondents;
4. confronting questions of *reciprocity* in field research and about the consequences of the research report on those who are studied.

My own thinking has been deeply influenced by the writings of Malinowski, Thomas and Znaniecki, the Chicago School, Dollard, the Lynds, Myrdal, and the many field workers who have recorded their research findings and procedures and raised deeply disturbing issues about the methods and direction of social science research. In this volume, illustrative case material will be drawn from many field work accounts, but I shall focus most fully on three experiences which clearly illuminate the major issues I intend to confront: William Foote Whyte's study of an American urban slum area,[1] Gerald D. Berreman's research in an Indian village,[2] and my own investigation of Chilean university students.[3] Elliot Liebow's study of *Tally's Corner*[4] is most pertinent to the first three chapters and will be discussed therein. Pierre L. van den Berghe's experiences in South Africa[5] illustrate the problems of gaining acceptance and adapting to the research setting and will be used in the first two chapters. Arlene Kaplan Daniels' work on American military life[6] will be discussed in Chapter I.

Other fascinating research reports, including Laud Humphreys' account of impersonal sex[7] and the Wichita jury investigation,[8] are crucial for the analysis of probing into sensitive areas of social life and will be discussed in Chapter III. Finally, Chapter IV, the section on reciprocity, draws upon the work of Arthur Vidich and Joseph Bensman,[9] A. Terry Rambo,[10] Lee Rainwater and David J. Pittman,[11] Oscar Lewis,[12] Michael Lewis,[13] Willard Gaylin,[14] Jane Cassels Record,[15] and others.[16]

In each of the many investigations cited above, the researcher played a somewhat distinctive role. Whyte, for example, attempted to participate fully in the life of Cornerville. He lived in the area, hung around the street corners, and yet endeavored to maintain sufficient detachment to analyze the complex system of social relations that characterized the community. Whyte utilized the methods of participant observation for the collection of his data.

Berreman, as an American anthropologist in a small Indian village, could never hope to achieve a similar degree of involvement. Rather, he strove to play the role of friendly and sympathetic "stranger." The good will and acceptance of local informants and respondents were absolutely essential to the success of his efforts for Berreman was vulnerable to the suspicion that he was in the service of outside and unfriendly interests. Berreman relied heavily on observation and informal interviews to collect his data and, unlike Whyte, was highly dependent on the service of a translator.

In Chile I was relatively uninvolved in the day-to-day activities of most of my respondents as I attempted to conduct a formal survey of the attitudes of a large sample of university students. Nonetheless, like Whyte and Berreman, I was vitally affected by their willingness to offer the hospitality accorded to friendly and sympathetic outsiders. Beyond this, I needed the active support of many student leaders able to supply information about the operation of their schools and willing to identify themselves as supporters of my project.

Although these three social scientists and the others whose works have been cited varied markedly in the extent of their involvement in the research setting, in the manner of their influence on their respondents, in the type of information they hoped to elicit, and in the research tools they utilized, they all confronted remarkably similar problems of field research. Each soon experienced the difficulties and challenges of gaining acceptance in a strange and often unfriendly environment, yet one in which an impressive number of people were willing to admit the "stranger" into their lives and confidence.[17]

## NOTES

1. William Foote Whyte, Appendix: "On the Evolution of Street Corner Society," *Street Corner Society* (Chicago: University of Chicago Press, 1955), pp. 279–358, paperback ed.

2. Gerald D. Berreman, *Behind Many Masks* (Ithaca, N.Y.: The Society for Applied Anthropology, 1962); and *Hindus of the Himalayas* (Berkeley: University of California Press, 1963).

3. Frank Bonilla and Myron Glazer, Appendix A: "A Note on Methodology. Field Work in a Hostile Environment: A Chapter in the Sociology of Social Research in Chile," *Student Politics in Chile* (New York: Basic Books, 1970), pp. 313–333.

4. Elliot Liebow, Appendix: "A Field Experience in Retrospect," *Tally's Corner* (Boston: Little, Brown, 1967), pp. 232–256.

5. Pierre L. van den Berghe, "Research in South Africa: The Story of My Experiences with Tyranny," in Gideon Sjoberg (ed.), *Ethics, Politics and Social Research* (Cambridge, Mass.: Schenkman, 1967), pp. 183–197.

6. Arlene Kaplan Daniels, "The Low-Caste Stranger in Social Research," in Sjoberg (ed.), *ibid.*, pp. 267–296.

7. Laud Humphreys, *Tearoom Trade* (Chicago: Aldine, 1970); and "Tearoom Trade: Impersonal Sex in Public Places," *Transaction* (January 1970), pp. 10–26.

8. *Recording of Jury Deliberations*, Hearings Before the Subcommittee to Investigate the Administration of the Internal Security Act and Other Internal Security Laws of the Committee on the Judiciary, United States Senate, Eighty-Fourth Congress, First Session, October 12 and 13, 1955. (Washington, D.C.: Government Printing Office, 1955).

9. Arthur Vidich and Joseph Bensman, *Small Town in Mass Society* (Princeton, N.J.: Princeton University Press, 1968).

10. The material discussing A. Terry Rambo's research experience in Vietnam is primarily drawn from personal correspondence between the author and Rambo during 1970–1971.

11. Lee Rainwater and David J. Pittman, "Ethical Problems in Studying a Politically Sensitive and Deviant Community," *Social Problems*, 14 (Spring 1967), 357–366.

12. Oscar Lewis, *La Vida* (New York: Random House, 1968).

13. Bernard Farber, David L. Harvey, and Michael Lewis, *Community, Kinship, and Competence*, Research and Development Program on Preschool Disadvantaged Children (Washington, D.C.: U.S. Department of Health, Education, and Welfare, 1969), Vol. III.

14. Willard Gaylin, *In the Service of Their Country/War Resisters in Prison* (New York: The Viking Press, 1970).

**15.** Jane Cassels Record, "The Research Institute and the Pressure Group," in Sjoberg (ed.), *op. cit.*, pp. 25–49.

**16.** For excellent analyses of many of the other aspects of the research process, consult Julian L. Simon, *Basic Research Methods in Social Science* (New York: Random House, 1969) and Norman K. Denzin, *The Research Act; A Theoretical Introduction to Sociological Methods* (Chicago: Aldine, 1970).

**17.** For accounts of field work in a wide variety of settings, see Morris Freilich (ed.), *Marginal Natives: Anthropologists at Work* (New York: Harper & Row, 1970). Also consult the Bibliography in this volume for other particularly useful reference material.

# CHAPTER I

# (A)

# gaining acceptance:
# defining the research and
# the researcher

In all research it is essential for the investigator to spend an initial period of time preparing the kinds of questions he wants to ask, developing his tools of data collection, and then venturing out and determining the extent to which his preconceived research design will fit into the actual field work situation. Gaining acceptance from informants and respondents is a crucial component of this process.

Every field worker immediately faces some form of resistance and suspicion. Regardless of the setting, prospective respondents and informants will be wary of the researcher's first overtures. They will want to know what kind of information he desires and how the accumulation of that knowledge will affect them. The researcher now faces his first set of field work challenges. How will he identify himself and his work? What changes will he have to make in his own attitudes and behavior in order to gain acceptance?

The investigator utilizes many approaches through which he hopes to vitiate suspicion, neutralize hostility, and garner support. Inherent in these is the field worker's declaration, implicit or explicit, that the respondents will receive something in return for assisting him. At times this is simply his gratitude, which may or may not be sufficient given the needs of the respondents and the personal attractiveness of the field worker. More often it is the investigator's declaration that he is deeply interested in the community and its people. Indeed, he may assert that their lives and struggles must be recorded so that others can benefit from their experiences. The researcher and his report will be their instrument. In making these declarations, the field worker will often promise things that he will later come to regret.

To reinforce his claim that he is sincerely interested in those he hopes to study, the researcher may occasionally want to assist respondents and informants in overcoming some of their immediate problems. This second line of relationship building may serve to undercut the doubts of the suspicious and enhance the position of those community members willing to accept the field worker on the basis of his personal assurances. Some form of *reciprocity*, then, is often essential in gaining acceptance.

When the field worker attempts to gain entrance into relatively closed communities, reciprocity alone may be insufficient. Other acts may also be necessary. The investigator may be hard-pressed to prove that his credentials are legitimate. Overt expressions of sympathy and appropriate acts of solidarity can be demanded as evidence that the field worker is unlikely to betray his informants. *Trust* is the crucial ingredient and may be more significant than the various forms of reciprocity.

When the field worker is unable to secure his position via reciprocity or trust, he may seek special prerogatives on the very basis that he is an outsider whose work necessitates that he trespass into normally restricted areas and relationships. The danger for the researcher here is that he may merely be *tolerated* and that he will be unable to call upon anyone in moments of crisis.

There are instances in which the researcher's appeals to reciprocity, trust, or tolerance, all prove ineffective. Potential informants may demand marked *alterations* in the field worker's demeanor and behavior to allay their fears, thus confronting the investigator with a problem of personal integrity.

Finally, there are important encounters in which the field worker fails to gain the acceptance he desires. Research projects carefully mapped in the security of the social scientist's office can founder when implementation is attempted. *Rejection* is always painful but may be valuable in demonstrating the realities of modern field research. Resistant respondents force the researcher, and, indeed, all his colleagues to reevaluate their assumptions of what they are about.

In essence, during the first stage of the field work adventure the researcher must make some difficult ethical decisions. How much should prospective informants and respondents be told about the exact nature of the project? To what extent is it permissible to make exaggerated claims about the researcher's ability to aid those he wants to study? Is the investigator justified in masking his critical views behind the guise of sympathetic interest? Researchers who practice subtle or overt deception in their desire to gain acceptance may often pay a heavy price when local people later ask for a return on their investment.

Understanding the process by which the field worker gains initial acceptance entails, then, a careful analysis of three major components of the research relationship: the research project and its appropriateness to the setting; the personality of the researcher and his ability to control his own anxiety during a period of uncertainty, as well as the many masks worn by him as he attempts to convince others that his work is worthy of respect and support; and the variety of respondents who will view the project and researcher according to their own perspectives and personality needs. Unraveling the complex acceptance process furnishes great insight into the research setting and into the field worker's role.


## CORNERVILLE

WHEREIN WHYTE MEETS DOC AND WINS HIS SUPPORT
BY RECOUNTING HIS DEEP INTEREST IN STUDYING
THE COMMUNITY AND BY SHOWING HIMSELF TO BE A
PERSON WHOSE FRIENDSHIP CAN BE VALUED.


The first appeal for acceptance by a field worker may stress his deep personal and scholarly interest in the people he wants to study. Beyond this he may assert that his efforts can help them gain the attention, understanding, and assistance of important public figures. This approach was particularly effective when made to struggling slum-dwellers during the Great Depression in the United States.

In the late 1930s William Foote Whyte was graduated from Swarthmore College.[1] He described himself as a young man concerned both with writing and social reform, but very much limited to his experiences in middle-class America. Indeed, despite what is considered an excellent educational background, including a year's study in Germany between high school and college, and though a leader in a number of campus controversies, Whyte modestly spoke of himself as a "very dull fellow." He particularly recalled his visits to the Philadelphia slums. There, he said, he felt like a conspicuous and inept tourist rather than a sophisticated and urbane observer. He applied for and won a prestigious fellowship from Harvard University, which allowed him to pursue any course of study for three years, and he decided to research a section of Boston.

At first Whyte thought of conducting a large-scale community survey. His plans entailed a study of the history of the district, its employment, housing, and marketing characteristics; its patterns of education, recreation, and church attendance; and, finally, a picture of its social attitudes. The effort, according to Whyte, would have involved the full-time services of ten investigators.

This ambitious plan was criticized by L. J. Henderson, the eminent and brilliant biochemist, who was secretary of the Harvard Society of Fellows that had awarded Whyte the fellowship. Hadn't Whyte proposed a large-scale study without sufficient exposure to the community? Wouldn't it be better to begin on a much smaller scale and then expand to include relevant questions?

Although initially deflated by these sharply worded queries, Whyte quickly found that the criticism was to the point. He reevaluated the project and decided to study intensively the social structure of the community. His reading of social science literature and discussions with professors and peers, particularly Conrad Arensberg, led him to focus on the objective patterns of interaction among the community's residents. Who contacts whom? How much time do they spend together? Who initiates the action? The community would be analyzed as an organized social system and not simply as an area containing social problems. Whyte sought to increase his understanding of a slum and to analyze the patterns of behavior that characterized its inhabitants. He rejected the view that social disorganization reigned in these areas. By participating in community life on a day-to-day basis, he could most readily test this major assertion.[2]

Whyte had embarked on what was to become a classic study of Cornerville. The pivotal problem of gaining entrance into the

community now had to be faced. He reports in vivid and amusing detail the fiasco of his initial efforts. A fellow student had
told him that he occasionally spent an evening by visiting a
local bar near Cornerville.' It was easy, he assured Whyte, to
drop in, offer to buy a woman a drink, and engage her in conversation about the area. Whyte seized upon the idea hoping
that he could make initial contact.

When he arrived at the bar the next evening, Whyte found
that all the women were in the company of men. Gathering his
courage, he approached a table where two women and a male
companion were engaged in conversation. He politely asked if
he could join the group. The man offered to throw Whyte down
a flight of stairs. Whyte beat a hasty retreat from both the
table and the bar. The problem of gaining acceptance still
remained.

Whyte next tried the local settlement house in Cornerville
itself. Surely the social workers there would understand his
needs and agree to help. He found, however, that the staff was
mixed in its reaction. Only one person showed any real enthusiasm, and she suggested that Whyte meet and explain his project
to a young local man who occasionally visited the settlement
house. Doc, she related, was precisely the kind of influential
person who could help in implementing the project.

The social worker's predictions were accurate. Doc listened
carefully to a description of the project and responded only
after Whyte had explained his sincere interest in studying the
people of the community and his desire to help them by writing
a book about Cornerville. Doc then offered to take Whyte to
visit any part of the area he wanted. Most important, he said
he would introduce Whyte as his friend. He was willing to provide Whyte with the first, and perhaps most essential, ingredient
of the field work effort—an identity for the investigator. Without that, as Whyte had already learned, the social scientist
would remain an unwelcome outsider suffering the anxiety pro-
duced by trying to gain entrance into a suspicious community.
Doc also offered to help by asking questions that would probe
areas of special interest.

Whyte had taken a giant step. In one brief encounter he had
gained a local identity and an invaluable informant who would
guide him through his first stumbling efforts.[3] We are never
told exactly why Doc responded so favorably. It seems evident,

however, that Doc saw Whyte as a sincere and attractive person, educated, and interested in the community. Whatever his exact reasons, Doc's standing was apparently secure enough to permit the introduction of a complete outsider as his good friend.

In spite of Doc's acceptance, Whyte was not completely in. Some hesitancy still remained about his intentions. A local newspaper editor confronted him with a series of questions about his activities. Whyte again had to explain what he was up to. His extensive notes are vague on the nature of his response in what must have been a tense situation. We are unclear what assurances he gave to his not unsympathetic interrogator. Yet we do know from Whyte's later statements that he was himself still quite vague about what he was after. He could only honestly assert that he was intent on writing a book and emphasized that he was sympathetic to the people of Cornerville, hoped to help them, and sincerely wanted them to like and to accept him. Whyte did not and no doubt could not tell the editor that he was going to make careful observations into people's lives and that Doc had agreed to help him probe into any activity that Whyte deemed important.

Most of the Cornerville residents whom he met later seemed willing to define Whyte's efforts according to their evaluation of *him*. If he were a good fellow, certainly he could bring no harm to the community. In the early stages of his research in Cornerville, Whyte was so preoccupied with gaining acceptance that most other questions faded into the background. It would be a long time before he would have to confront directly the legitimate demands for reciprocity that would be made by certain local people who would blanch at Whyte's ultimate portrayal of them.

Whyte's early days in Cornerville reveal how exposed and dependent most field workers are until they establish an acceptable place for themselves within the community. Because of his vulnerable position, the field worker is deeply appreciative of minor kindness and often overwhelmed by those genuinely able and willing to assist him. Field workers often interpret acceptance as a reaffirmation of their own worth, particularly if it occurs after some ego damaging experiences. Thus, Doc's friendship was an essential and timely symbol of the legitimacy of Whyte's study and a crucial prop for Whyte's highly insecure definition of himself as a competent field worker. Most investigators desperately need those who will nurture their still fragile sense of mastering an uncertain situation.

The early informants, then, play a dual role. They alert the researcher to the realities of the situation under study and provide him with an entrée. They also, and perhaps just as important, help cement the researcher's identity during those trying moments when the field worker is unsure both of himself and of the direction his own work is taking. It is not uncommon for the social scientist to develop and nourish an abiding debt of gratitude for the kindness shown him during the early days in the field.

As a result, certain questions arise. Researchers like William Whyte eventually ponder the ethical limits of their scholarly responsibilities. Their informants often willingly expose their own vulnerabilities to their new "friend" in the faith that they and their community will not be hurt. Yet, even the researcher who is deeply concerned about the sensitivities of his hosts is committed to tell the story as he sees it. How can anyone understand Cornerville without exploring some of its less positive aspects? How can Doc and his friends be understood if you only see their strengths? Whyte ultimately would have to answer these and other troubling questions.


## TALLY'S CORNER

WHEREIN LIEBOW, WHO GREW UP IN A PREDOMINANTLY
BLACK NEIGHBORHOOD, ACTS OUT HIS FRIENDSHIP BY
HELPING LONNY FACE A MURDER CHARGE AND GAINS
THE TRUST OF TALLY AND THE OTHER BLACK MEN.


While Whyte emphasized his deep interest in Cornerville and spoke of his belief that his book might help its residents, other researchers have been more direct in building their initial relationships on more concrete forms of reciprocity. A prime example of this situation occurred in Elliot Liebow's study of black workingmen in Washington, D.C., conducted in the early 1960s.[4] This research also utilized the method of participant observation. Liebow's task was to gather information to contribute to a larger study of "Child Rearing Practices Among Low-Income

Families in the District of Columbia." His goal was to focus on the family, friendship, and work lives of the black underemployed men. He wanted to understand how they spend their time when off the job; the nature of their relationships with wives, girl friends, children, and peers; and their methods of adapting to their pleasures and problems. Like Whyte, Liebow did not set forth any clear hypotheses to be tested. Rather, he felt that it was extremely important to study black men in their own environments fully and in great detail. Too often, he felt, information about them had been garnered from the records of those who had come into contact with the authorities. This, Liebow believed, led to a particular kind of biased and superficial account. Participant observation would more effectively remedy and supplement the paucity of previous material than the more formal and partial techniques of questionnaire and interviewing.[5]

Liebow strongly believed that his study could shed important light on the men's lives and struggles and thus affect social policy to their advantage. Unlike some social scientists only a few years later, Liebow did not believe that the information he gathered would be used to reenforce the negative image held by many Americans about lower-class ghetto blacks. In the early 1960s, social scientists, as well as many blacks, still firmly believed in white-black cooperation and hoped that government policy could be effectively influenced by the penetrating arguments of social scientists who told it like it was.

Hylan Lewis, the study director and an important consultant throughout the research, indicated a potentially interesting part of the city, and Liebow simply made his way down one of the streets. Although not black and now a middle-class professional, he felt less trepidation in making initial contact than had Whyte. Liebow had grown up in working class areas and had had far greater contact with the kinds of people he hoped to study.

Liebow's first encounters were quite informal. He shared some observations with several men about the dramatic arrest of a local woman by a reputedly hard-nosed detective. The next day Liebow and several others catered to the needs of a hungry puppy, and it was then that he met Tally Jackson. Afterward they spent several hours in a carry-out restaurant talking mostly about Tally, but also about Liebow's job. During the next few weeks Liebow met a number of the other local men and slowly began to shake off the feeling of strangeness. He felt more at ease, a little less the outsider on the block. But suspicion remained. There was still insufficient evidence that Liebow was trustworthy, that he really had a right to be around.

The turning point came several weeks after Liebow's first appearance. Lonny, one of the local men, had been indicted for the murder of his wife, and Tally had been subpoenaed to appear in court in his defense. Because it was late and Tally had no money for a taxi, Liebow offered him a ride to the courthouse. From that moment on, the walls that separated the social scientist from the black man crumbled as Liebow became an active participant. Both Lonny and Tally began to look toward him for advice as Liebow became Lonny's unofficial legal counsel. Others frequenting the corner carry-out restaurant inquired as to Lonny's well-being. Liebow became identified as a friend who had come through in a moment of crisis. It was known that he had been at various trials and hearings, had spoken to a variety of public officials on Lonny's behalf, and had been accepted by Lonny's family.

In addition, Tally and Liebow were now "real tight." Tally indicated that he stood ready to help Liebow in any way possible. To set their relationship absolute straight, Tally confessed about lying during their first meeting. Though he feared that Liebow might hold it against him, Tally said he wanted no deception to mar their friendship.

Liebow's increased acceptance was also revealed in other ways. The local numbers man began calling him by his first name and now took bets in his presence. Newcomers to the neighborhood came to Liebow with questions. Liebow was someone who had been around and who was in the know.

Important barriers, of course, remained. Color was the most crucial and obvious. Liebow perceptively records that when he was part of a group of four, he saw three black men. Each of the others observed two blacks and a white. He could never overcome this difference. Yet, Liebow put the barrier in some perspective. He depicted the separation as if it were a "chain-linked fence." As two people moved closer to it, they saw less of the metallic divider and more of the unique characteristics of each other.

Liebow, who had come as an outsider, had won acceptance by his willingness to lend a helping hand in time of trouble. His arently sincere interest in the men had been acted out rather than spoken. Color and social class differences, while real, were seen as becoming less important than the growing bonds of friendship. Liebow had clearly indicated that his presence posed no threat to any of the men. On the contrary, he could be relied upon in a moment of need. He stood ready to reciprocate as a friend in a direct and vital way in exchange for the acceptance that he sought.

Like Whyte, Liebow's highly successful efforts to win acceptance in the black community raise a number of significant questions. What are the limits of "humanitarianism" and "sympathy" when employed by the field worker? Are researchers sincere when we offer help to those we want to study? Or do we usually put ourselves at the service of others only as long as they have information which we hope to secure?

## CHILE

WHEREIN I APPEAL FOR AND SECURE THE HELP OF FELLOW
UNIVERSITY STUDENTS, BUT SOON LEARN THAT SUSPICION
IS UBIQUITOUS AND MUST BE CONFRONTED HEAD-ON.

The researcher's ability to gain acceptance through the appeal of reciprocity is facilitated when informants define the research project itself as contributing in a very real way to the achievement of their own goals. This is clearly the situation when politically active men and women are approached for their cooperation. They often balance out the costs of assisting the field worker intent on probing into sensitive areas against the gains that they can legitimately expect for their own cause. The balance is particularly delicate when the researcher comes from a powerful nation whose support is desired but whose policies and good will are continually suspect. In this tense situation the appeal to reciprocity will need to be supplemented by a strong injection of trust in the integrity of the researcher. Only this ingredient can facilitate entrance into situations that are normally closed to outsiders.

In 1963 my wife, Penina, and I arrived in Santiago, Chile, to study the professional and political attitudes of Chilean university students.[6] Several years earlier I had conducted a study of American graduate students in physics. The research had focused on their incipient professional self-concepts and had tried to understand how the norms of the scientific community were passed on to neophytes through the graduate school experience. Later, I became intrigued by the dual roles that many Latin American university students are called upon to play. Their dramatic activities in national upheavals had been graphically described in the press and in scholarly studies dealing with their political involvement. I was interested in the experiences of the rank and file of students preparing for future professional careers and the impact on them of university, national, and international political events. I hoped to interview a large sample of students preparing for a variety of professional careers and to determine the relationship that exists between the professional and political roles of university students. Perhaps most important, I was deeply sympathetic to the thousands of Latin American students who had risked career and life in the struggle for social justice. I wanted to know some of them and hoped that I could contribute to their struggle through my research.

It was immediately apparent that the complex political alignments in the University of Chile could seriously affect our work. No attempt to interview a large number of students could be successful without consent from all the major student political groups. Tacit approval from student leaders would be insufficient. Contacts were needed to help obtain lists of enrolled students, to arrange meeting places, and to encourage active cooperation. It was absolutely essential to secure the assistance of student activists from all the major leftwing parties in the highly politicized university in order to interview several hundred of their peers.

We knew how suspicious these students could be of North Americans, particularly of their interest during the year of a crucial and closely contested Chilean presidential election. Events in Guatemala in 1954 and in Cuba only two years before provided firm basis for potential accusations that we were agents hostile to any leftwing victory. It was, therefore, vitally important to identify ourselves as sympathetic graduate students, supported only by the private Doherty Foundation and having no connection with the United States Embassy, the C.I.A., or other United States government agencies.

We had been given a letter of introduction to the director

of a social science training institute sponsored by the United Nations. He was a friend of my adviser at Princeton University and was most cordial in his welcome. The director listened carefully to my description of our proposed research and predicted that we would have difficulty winning the friendship and cooperation of the leftwing student groups. He suggested that we contact a Chilean social scientist active in the Socialist party who might be willing to introduce us to student activists. We soon found ourselves having dinner at this man's house. He had also invited two Socialist party student leaders, Jaime and Roberto, to meet us, and we spent a delightful evening drinking good Chilean wine, singing folksongs, and talking politics.

Our acceptance was no doubt facilitated by a sense of comradeship fostered by our role as university students. We knew the problems faced by those Chileans trying to define themselves in relation to major national issues. We were familiar with the American magazines that the Chilean students read and admired. We were able to inform them about what was happening on college campuses in the United States, what direction the civil rights struggle was taking, and what the basis of United States policy toward Cuba appeared to be. The Chilean students were obviously pleased to meet North Americans with whom they could discuss a wide variety of issues.

As a result of that first evening, we decided to ask the student leaders whether they would be willing to help us with the study. We were apprehensive that, though they had welcomed us warmly, they might be reluctant to support our research effort publicly. We were well aware of the great rivalry that existed between the Socialist students and their Communist allies on one side and the Christian Democratic students on the other. We feared that our Socialist friends would hesitate because of the suspicions of the Communists or the criticisms of the Christian Democrats. Close public association with North Americans could prove embarrassing.

As Whyte had explained his project to Doc, so we spoke of our interest in Chilean student life. Roberto and Jaime quickly assured us that they would introduce us to their peers and assist us in any other way necessary. They agreed that the project could be of help to both Chileans and North Americans interested in better understanding student attitudes on many important issues. Our friends obviously respected the importance of scholarly study in facilitating social change. They wanted others to know about Chile's deep-rooted social problems and their faith in the Socialists' efforts to confront them.

We now faced the problem of winning the support of the Communist and Christian Democratic students. I was first introduced to Christian Democratic student leaders in one of the school cafeterias as I was having coffee with the Socialists. When I met with the Christian Democrats later in the day, I sensed a certain reserve. The introduction had only served to arouse their suspicions. They had associated me with their opponents. The Christian Democrats had to be convinced of my motives and of my reasons for studying political questions. Penina and I managed to overcome the initial difficulty by carefully explaining our interests. Most of these young men were impressed by the seriousness of doctoral research and were quite helpful and supportive in moments of subsequent crisis. Our feeling persisted, however, that a few continued to remain somewhat aloof precisely because we had not cultivated their friendship first.

The first Communist students we met were openly cool in their attitude. They questioned us very closely about our own views, especially toward Cuba and United States policy in Latin America. Where it was warranted, we criticized the United States and its often rigid and short-sighted policies. We also insisted that the ruling groups and all political parties in Latin America bear their share of the responsibility for existing problems. In addition, we continued to emphasize, no doubt in vain, that these students really knew little about life and politics in the United States. We repeatedly stressed the complexity of the situation and rejected a monolithic caricature. We were never warmly embraced by the Communists, and this failure was to haunt us later.

At the same time, we tried to convince *all* the Chilean student leaders that we wanted to understand their positions, that our study merited their active support, and that it could make contributions toward the United States' knowledge of Chile's problems. We knew that this appeal most directly met the reciprocity expectations of the activists. All were committed to the attainment of national political power through legal means. Most, like Ana María, the medical student daughter of an important political figure in the leftwing coalition whom I had met through Jaime, hoped that their positive program could sway public opinion in the United States. Ana María was willing to put all of her prestige behind our request to interview students in the medical school. Through her enthusiastic support, we were later able to gain the acceptance and cooperation of key student leaders in her own Socialist group and among Christian Democrats and independents in the School of Medicine. Her trust was far more influential there than any appeal to reciprocity that we were able to make.

The Chilean activist students, like Ana María, hoped that President John F. Kennedy had the imagination, flexibility, and good will to recognize the need for sweeping change in Chile. They saw studies like ours as contributing toward that end; there was mutual benefit to be derived from our growing friendship. Six months later, after President Kennedy had been assassinated and after the Brazilian military coup had taken place, student leaders began to doubt seriously whether their hopes for United States government understanding could ever be realized. These events were to have a devastating impact on our research.

Our success in gaining the cooperation and friendship of Chilean student leaders raised a number of difficult questions that we had to answer upon our return to the United States. Was it appropriate for us to appeal to students as peers and colleagues? Were our commitments really the same as theirs? What likelihood was there that our work could contribute to a better understanding of Chile's problems by our countrymen and government? Moreover, was it appropriate for us to camouflage our sympathy for the socialists by feigning political neutrality while encouraging our informants to be honest and open with us? Don't informants have a right and need to know the researchers' value commitments and political views?

# (B)

# suspicion intensified

The diverse cases just discussed reveal that field workers must break through the walls of suspicion that surround any stranger. Barriers may be reduced by the growing bonds of friendship, by the immediate reciprocity inherent in specific and observable acts, or by meeting the political needs of respondents.

Other field work accounts show, however, that suspicion will stiffen if the field worker is labeled as a dangerous outsider. Residents of small isolated villages or the oppressed in an authoritarian regime may quickly identify the field worker as a police spy whose presence can have severe repercussions for them. Similarly, male military officers may readily associate a female, civilian professional with hostile outsiders intent on ruthlessly exposing and condemning them. Under certain circumstances social scientists themselves may accuse their own colleagues of being agents of a foreign power. Cooperation may be defined as a betrayal of national as well as scholarly interests.

Investigators who are unable to counter suspicions about what they are after or whom they represent are doomed to failure. It is not unknown for research projects to founder during the earliest stages of the field work effort because suspicion is not adequately overcome.

[25]

## INDIA

WHEREIN BERREMAN FACES MARKED RESISTANCE UNTIL HE
SPEAKS PASSIONATELY ABOUT THE VILLAGE'S GROWING
IMPORTANCE TO PEOPLE IN INDIA AND THE UNITED STATES AND
THEREBY WINS A MORE ATTENTIVE HEARING FROM THOSE
GRATIFIED BY NATIONAL AND INTERNATIONAL STATURE.

While some field workers ask potential respondents to accept
them as friends or perform concrete acts revealing their concern for the well-being of local people, other investigators must
overcome the severe suspicion often reserved for foreigners.
In Chile, Penina and I successfully gained the support of student activists because they viewed our work as contributing to
the realization of their political goals. People living in isolated
villages, however, are less familiar with the researcher's role
and quite readily define all strangers as a direct threat. The
field worker must find an appeal that makes sense to those he
seeks to study. This effort may take several months during
which time marked hostility meets the researcher's efforts to
gain acceptance. The field worker's effectiveness in overcoming
insulating walls of suspicion can be enhanced by his uncover-
ing the particular reciprocity needs of potential respondents
and then claiming that he is able to meet them through the
vehicle of his research.

Gerald D. Berreman employed this approach in his study of
a small and isolated peasant village in the lower Himalayas of
North India. Discussing the aims of his doctoral research and
the reasons for selecting this particular village, Berreman stated
that he wanted "... to analyze the functioning and interrelation-
ship of kin, caste, and community ties ... [and] to study the
effects of recent governmental programs and other outside
contacts on a relatively isolated and conservative Indian community." His reasons for selecting the village of Sirkanda were
both practical and scholarly. The village "... was fairly isolated
but accessible, had a caste distribution typical of the area, and
had no apparent important atypical features."[7] It was located
near the town of Dehra Dun where Berreman knew an interpreter and could find housing and medical services for his wife
and small daughter.

In an isolated village of 384 people any outsider immediately becomes the object of suspicion. The villagers of the region, Berreman reports, had a reputation for nonfriendliness, and teachers and public officials alike were treated with hostility. Strangers had only come to collect taxes and extort bribes, and, since independence in 1948, restrictive government regulations had increased. The villagers knew they were vulnerable to charges of illegal use of national forest lands, failure to register fire arms properly, desertion from army service, illegal use of land left by fleeing Muslims, and allowing children to marry below the legal age. Villagers also feared those who might accuse them of lack of religious orthodoxy, abduct their women, or force them into complicated and costly legal battles. Strangers, in short, were defined as real threats over whom very little social control could be exercised. As nonmembers of the local community, strangers were not subject to its regulations. Their actions were unpredictable and thus highly suspect and threatening.

The researcher not only had to face these barriers, but also had to confront an internal system of rigid caste stratification. The village was divided between the high castes and the low or untouchable castes. The high castes dominated political power and economic wealth as well as social prestige. The low castes owned little land, were primarily artisans, and were dependent for their livelihood on the high castes. The high castes comprised about 90 percent of the population. Acceptance by their group did not assure cooperation by the other.

Berreman and his young high-caste assistant, Sharma, arrived in the village in September 1957. They carried a letter of introduction from a merchant to a leading high-caste villager. The note asked that the strangers be received with hospitality. This proved to be the almost instantaneous undoing of the research effort. The merchant who provided the introduction had acquired a reputation for dishonest dealings with the villagers. The man to whom it was addressed was one of the most suspicious people in the village. Berreman quickly discovered that acceptance would not be won easily. The villagers believed that the anthropologists were missionaries, or government officials intent on raising taxes, or military recruiters, or even foreign spies.

The turning point came one afternoon, three months after the researchers arrived in the village, when a hostile village leader interrupted an interview and demanded to know why certain questions were being asked. As a crowd quickly gathered, Berreman sensed the opportunity to reduce suspicion about his efforts. He explained that his presence and his questions directly reflected the growing importance of the village in international events. Before Indian independence, the American government simply dealt with the British. Now, as a sign of the importance of Indian-American relations, each country exchanged hundreds of students to study the language, customs, and religion of the other. This was absolutely essential if the countries were to deal justly with one another. In this effort, the part of the country in which the village was located had been overlooked. As a beautiful and historic area it would surely become central in India's development. It was important, then, that India and the outer world know more about the area and its people.

This strongly worded and emotional answer had its impact. Few of the villagers had ever heard Berreman speak at length, and they responded sympathetically to his appeal for understanding and assistance. He felt that they knew him well enough by this time to allow themselves to be convinced by his speech. Berreman's obvious appeal to the villagers' sense of self-worth emphasized the benefits they would derive from his stay. He was sensitive to their feeling that they were held in low esteem and constantly disparaged by neighboring plains people. He was not simply asking for cooperation but would help put their village on the map of national affairs and international relations.

Berreman had adroitly maneuvered his hosts into an uncomfortable position. Overt hostility could now be interpreted as callous disregard for the village's standing. Berreman had successfully begun to manage the image that others held of the work that he and Sharma were engaged in. Like Whyte, he had begun to convince his hosts that he had come to do them no harm, rather that there were benefits to be gained by his presence. As we were about our research in Chile, he was explicit about the type of political returns to be expected from his stay. Berreman had effectively used the appeal of reciprocity to break down the villagers' hostility toward outsiders. According to his description, they became more willing to judge him as a man rather than as a foreigner and outsider. Berreman did not, however, alert them to the extent to which he would probe into the most sensitive areas of local life. The villagers would learn this only after the field workers had become virtual fixtures in the village, never warmly embraced but at least tolerated by its people.

Several less dramatic but equally important events facilitated Berreman's and Sharma's initial acceptance. As single men, they had been defined as a threat to village women. The visit to the village by their wives and children greatly diminished this suspicion. They also won good will by suggesting simple medical remedies and by making their radio available to the villagers. The villagers also carefully checked Sharma's claims to Brahmin birth by visiting his city home.

In all, the villagers, some grudgingly and reluctantly, came to accept the presence of the visitors and the legitimacy of their research efforts. As with so many things in their lives, the villagers believed that it was fated that Berreman and Sharma should come to live with them. Indeed, Berreman observes that this explanation was as reasonable as any that he could provide as to why he had chosen to study this particular village. The researchers had finally achieved an acceptable identity. This was a first and vital step. Many other difficult problems would soon have to be overcome.

Berreman's method in winning the cooperation of the suspicious villagers again raises the ethical issue of the proper limits of our appeals to informants. Berreman clearly exaggerated the prospective benefits of his study when he claimed that he would put Sirkanda "on the map." What were his responsibilities to the villagers as people rather than as sources of data? Did he have the right to force them to be honest and open while he behaved in a self-conscious and calculating manner? Recently, Berreman and other anthropologists have begun to give far more serious consideration to these questions.


## SOUTH AFRICA

WHEREIN VAN DEN BERGHE CONFRONTS THE REALITIES OF
APARTHEID AND SEEKS THE TOLERANCE OF THE OPPRESSED BY
IGNORING THE RESTRICTIVE AND DEMEANING SEPARATIST REGULATIONS.

In a highly coercive social system, the researcher is often unable to convince the oppressed of his good will. They have much to lose through betrayal. Where intergroup understanding has been irreparably damaged, the promise of reciprocity has lost its most essential underpinning. The appeal to trust is similarly ineffective. The researcher can at best struggle to prove his separateness from the subjugating powers and hope that the underdogs, while ever wary, will grow tolerant of his presence and questions.

In the early 1960s, Pierre L. van den Berghe, an American sociologist of Belgian and French descent, arrived in the Union of South Africa to study its apartheid system. The white government has determined that this is the most appropriate method by which the white minority can maintain its racial purity, its political power, its economic advantage, and its social prestige. Van den Berghe decided that he would not inform the government of his actual research goals but instead announced that he was interested in studying South Africa's booming economy. The authorities accepted his explanation. Van den Berghe feels that as a consequence of their general inefficiency they interfered little with his work.

Van den Berghe faced great difficulties in attempting to gain the cooperation of nonwhites. The apartheid policy had not only segregated the races physically, it had also created an atmosphere of intense suspicion. Why should Van den Berghe be trusted? Wasn't he a white man? Didn't a high official in the police have a surname that sounded remarkably similar to his? Didn't Van den Berghe drive a beige Volkswagon, which was the car utilized by the "special branch" of the police? Van den Berghe quickly learned that the social scientist is only partially in control of his own role definition. Under the best of circumstances, interracial relations were extremely difficult to maintain.

Van den Berghe found that educated and militant Africans defined him as a police agent, a do-gooder, or a missionary. Older and more traditional Africans were more cautious and subservient in their contacts with him, a response that hindered his ability to establish open communications with them. As with Berreman, others attempted to fit him into previously defined roles and responded accordingly. Similar to our experience with the Communist students in Chile, antagonism based on political factors created an immediate barrier.

Van den Berghe's most complete failure occurred in his attempt to conduct interviews among migrant agricultural workers. They belonged to the Pondo subgroup of the Xhosa and were at the time (early 1961) in open revolt against the South African government. In Van den Berghe's presence, his African assistant conducted a series of fifteen-minute interviews. Van den Berghe observed that the respondents answered the factual questions slowly and sullenly and gave noncommittal replies when asked to evaluate their attitudes toward whites. When Van den Berghe was not present, however, the respondents vehemently denounced the whites and decried the bondage in which they lived. Most significantly, word immediately spread to surrounding communities not to cooperate with the study. As a result, Van den Berghe's assistant reported a 100 percent refusal rate. The government had recently attempted to conduct a census in Pondoland that also had been effectively boycotted. The workers had no reason to doubt that Van den Berghe and his assistant were government agents.

Many whites were equally critical of Van den Berghe's actions and attitudes but for entirely different reasons. Some quickly defined him as a communist agitator. Others were less angered and more amused by his "naïveté" in dealing with the "natives." They maintained that he would quickly learn how appropriate their system of apartheid was.

In sum, Van den Berghe experienced far greater difficulties in defining his role than the other social scientists we have discussed. In a society built upon coercion and mistrust, there is less likelihood that the "stranger" will be accepted by any of the competing groups. Legal sanctions precluded, or at least made difficult, the establishment of informal interracial contacts. Had Van den Berghe studied only the white community, he would have avoided some of the conflict situations. As someone who desired access to all groups, however, he was constantly stepping across boundaries into dangerous areas:

I became known as a white person who shook hands with nonwhites and called them "Mr." or "Mrs.," invited them to my house in Durban, and accepted hospitality from them even to the extent of sitting at the same dining table with them and using their toilet facilities, both highly polluting acts in the scale of white South African racial phobias. Edna Miller, my assistant, was in the same position, but much of her field work consisted of interviewing whites, a job which

I often found so unpleasant that I selfishly delegated it to her. Though an American by birth and a liberal by conviction, she had lived in South Africa for ten years, and she did not mind too much. In fact, some of her best friends were whites![8]

Van den Berghe's reaction was to attempt to ignore all the apartheid regulations possible and to risk harassment and arrest. While the role of social scientist afforded him very few special liberties, the role of unknowledgeable "stranger" served as sufficient protection during the most dangerous transgressions. He was able to move more freely than would otherwise have been possible in restricted areas and to treat nonwhites more in accord with the dictates of his conscience. In this way he was simultaneously able to win limited cooperation from the oppressed majority of Africans and to maintain his own sense of integrity. Van den Berghe was to pay a heavy price, however, for his determination to remain in South Africa.

Van den Berghe gained access to South Africa by pretending to be interested in its booming economy rather than its racial policies. He consciously deceived the government which granted him a visa. He lived in constant fear that his real intentions would be discovered and that he would be expelled. What are our ethical commitments when we are tolerated guests in foreign countries? Are we justified in deceiving the "gatekeepers" who can permit or withhold access? Do we have one set of responsibilities to South Africa or Portugal and another to Yugoslavia or Cuba? Yet should we be completely honest when such honesty would lead to exclusion?

## THE AMERICAN MILITARY

WHEREIN DANIELS MEETS INITIAL REJECTION AND LEARNS THAT
MALE MILITARY OFFICERS WILL TRUST A FEMALE CIVILIAN PROFESSIONAL
ONLY WHEN SHE IS SYMPATHETIC AND SUBMISSIVE.

There are situations in which respondents will reject the appeals of reciprocity, trust, or tolerance and will insist that the researcher perform according to their definition of appropriate behavior. When this occurs, the investigator is confronted with one of the most problematic aspects in the first phase of the field work endeavor. How appropriate are the demands that respondents make? What alterations by the researcher in his manifest attitudes and behavior are consistent with the maintenance of his own integrity?

Arlene Kaplan Daniels is a sociologist who was interested in studying army life.[9] As a woman professional seeking access to a closed system commanded by men, she suffered a series of humiliating setbacks. Her experiences reveal the significance of sex, occupational, and personality differences in gaining acceptance.[10]

Daniels set out to study the life situations of new army recruits undergoing basic training. Although she had permission from high-level military officials, she quickly found, like Berreman, that officials are not always respected or trusted at the local level and that the success or failure of her research depended upon her acceptance by liaison officers, who were resentful of her forceful professional manner, her civilian status, and her sex. A firm handshake, a straightforward look in the eye, and a cheerful disposition were defined as inappropriate and disrespectful behavior in a woman civilian. She realized that her military associates defined her role according to *their* precepts of appropriate conduct. They rejected, sometimes indirectly and often boldly, her attempts to present herself as a competent professional who, as director of the study, could command their help. Both the researcher and the others were committed to defining her emerging role in a manner suitable to their own views.

Daniels made it clear that she had a contract from the Army to do a research project and that she expected the kind of respect and cooperation accorded to any professional. She was confident of her ability and, at first, simply assumed that the officers would assist her as part of their jobs. She was unaware that she and her mandate were being questioned at every step. Daniels openly stated that she had secured a three-year commitment from high-level military authorities in Washington. The officers interpreted this as a weak obligation since only five- and ten-year terms were considered as serious. In addition, the local officer who had initially voiced deep interest in her research proved concerned only as long as an expression of interest served to prevent his unwanted transfer.

Daniels' problems of acceptance and identification became even more acute when she changed her study from basic trainees to the military organization of the base itself. Now she needed more active assistance from the officers who saw her data gathering as a direct threat to their everyday work lives. Some simply and directly asked why they should cooperate with her efforts. She was an outsider who obviously had little commitment to them or their way of operating. Why should they expend their own time to give her information that might very well be used against them?

The researcher was advised by an officer who had befriended her to change her style of behavior drastically:

> Most galling (to them) of all was my naïve assumption that, *of course*, I was equal. It was important to wait until equality was *given* me. When I learned to smile sweetly, keep my eyes cast down, ask helplessly for favors, and exhibit explicitly feminine mannerisms, my ability to work harmoniously and efficiently increased. Close and, for me, somewhat exaggerated attention to feminine behavior paid off because it showed I was willing to be a "good nigger." I learned the equivalents of the tugged forelock, the shuffle, and the "yassuh boss" of other minority groups.[11]

Daniels' change in behavior was also associated with several important insights that both enabled her to win the acceptance of her military respondents and to understand more fully their behavior and attitudes. She had begun her study with a set of highly critical and derogatory attitudes about life in the military and had initially assumed that career officers were less competent than their civilian professional counterparts. If they were not, why would they have chosen a career in the service? Her prospective informants were aware of her attitude and responded in a predictably defensive manner. They were sensitive to the status issue and they refused to expose themselves to a "sharp-tongued" critic writing an "exposé." They would only discuss their problems with someone basically sympathetic to their situation.

While it is often appropriate for the researcher to assume a neutral stance, this is seldom productive in establishing rapport with suspicious respondents. At a minimum, the military officers wanted to be reassured that Daniels understood them. Her protestations of professional neutrality were less important than her respect and appreciation of the difficult tasks they had to perform. She had to establish an identity as a sympathetic and knowledgeable civilian who could be trusted.

Understanding and interest could be evinced in a number of ways. Daniels learned many of the technical details of the officers' work. She read military journals carefully and expressed "knowledgeable" appreciation of her respondents' problems. Thus, with her changed attitude toward her own role, her greater respect of military expertise, and her expression of sympathetic understanding, Daniels became valued as a listener. Many of her respondents granted her interviews because they enjoyed talking about their work. Others did so because it enabled them to rethink their own work procedures. Many exploited her for her knowledge of doings at other bases, of who had transferred, resigned, divorced, or married. Reciprocity in information sharing became a central component of the research relationship. She was defined as a person "in the know."

Solidifying personal relationships was the final method by which she gained an appropriate identity. Since much of the interviewing had to occur after work hours so as not to disturb office procedures, Daniels had to persuade respondents to spend some of their free time with her. This aim was often accomplished by befriending the officers' families and being invited to social engagements. In this manner Daniels was also able to gather information from the officers' wives. Most important, data gathered at formal interview sessions could be corroborated at the more informal meetings.

The creation of some warm personal relationships was the culmination of the long, hard struggle to win acceptance. A significant point was reached when an officer explained Daniels' presence by telling a friend that she was the company "mascot." In a manner suggestive of the Indian villager who announced to a traveler that Berreman "lived" in the village, the officer indicated that they had "adopted" the investigator. She was one of the group who, within certain limited areas and in a subordinate status, was privy to insights and information that were withheld from the outsider.

Daniels ultimately gained access to the military community

by establishing an identity as a sympathetic researcher. She did so with the intention of analyzing Army institutions in a critical and forceful manner. What are the limits on the field worker's image manipulation? How does this differ from the constant image manipulation we all engage in as part of our daily lives? Are we constrained to be more sensitive to this issue when our efforts will result in a published document? Are we justified in deceiving military officers but not welfare recipients because the former have more defenses available to them? What are our responsibilities to military personnel as people rather than as informants?

## PROJECT CAMELOT

WHEREIN NUTTINI, FORMER CHILEAN CITIZEN AND
REPRESENTATIVE OF A $6 MILLION STUDY OF REVOLUTION, IS
CONDEMNED BY CHILEAN SOCIAL SCIENTISTS CRITICAL OF THE
UNITED STATES ARMY SPONSORSHIP AND LEARNS THE STUFF OF
WHICH INTERNATIONAL SCANDALS ARE MADE.

Under certain circumstances no appeal to reciprocity, trust, or tolerance is effective. And no definition or redefinition of the researcher's role or project can elicit any sympathetic interest from informants. They simply and unequivocally state their total hostility to the field worker and his project. He is firmly informed that there is no possibility of his building an appropriate role.

The process of gaining acceptance is brought into sharper focus when we examine an instance in which the investigator failed to secure the necessary cooperation. A highly significant and dramatic example of rejection occurred in Santiago, Chile, in April 1965, a few weeks before the United States landed Marines in the Dominican Republic. Hugo Nuttini, a former Chilean citizen and, at that time, an anthropologist on the faculty of the University of Pittsburgh, introduced himself to a number of Chilean social scientists as the representative of a large-scale multicountry research project focusing on the causes of revolution. Project Camelot, he assured them, was sponsored by several well-known private American foundations. Nuttini sought to enlist the Chileans as local collaborators.

The Chilean social scientists were suspicious and critical. They confronted Nuttini with a copy of the Project Camelot research proposal. This statement clearly set forth the project's research aims and its sponsorship by the United States Army. According to the project statement, the objectives of the study were:

*First:* to devise procedures for assessing the potential for internal war within national societies.

*Second:* to identify with increased degrees of confidence those actions which a government might take to relieve conditions which are assessed as giving rise to potential for internal war.

*Finally:* to assess the feasibility of prescribing the characteristics of a system for obtaining and using the essential information needed for doing the above two things.[12]

The statement continued with an emphasis on the growing and legitimate interest of the American defense establishment in

... the social processes which must be understood in order to deal effectively with problems of insurgency. Within the Army there is especially ready acceptance of the need to improve the general understanding of the processes of social change if the Army is to discharge its responsibilities in the over-all counterinsurgency program of the U.S. Government.[13]

Earlier in the document, the project's designers described its history:

By way of background: Project Camelot is an outgrowth of the interplay of many factors and forces. Among these is the assignment in recent years of much additional emphasis to the U.S. Army's role in the over-all U.S. policy of encouraging steady growth and change in the less developed countries in the world. The many programs of the U.S. Government directed toward this objective are often grouped under the sometimes misleading label of counterinsurgency. . . . This places great importance on positive actions designed to reduce the sources of disaffection which often give rise to more conspicuous and violent activities disruptive in nature. The U.S. Army has an important mission in the positive and constructive aspects of nation building as well as a responsibility to assist friendly governments in dealing with active insurgency problems.[14]

The document had been circulated in Chile by a Norwegian sociologist, Johan Galtung, who had been asked to serve as a consultant. Galtung rejected the lucrative offer and condemned the project as another attempt by the United States military to intervene in the internal affairs of Latin American countries. He had made his accusations known to a number of Chilean colleagues who flatly refused to assist Nuttini. Nuttini's clumsy attempt to disguise the sponsorship had simply confirmed their view that Project Camelot had no social science legitimacy.

The Camelot issue quickly reached national and then international proportions. Members of the Chilean Senate were informed of the incident, and they condemned the United States. All sectors of the Chilean press excoriated the project in banner headlines, asserting that no social scientist could use their country to further the mission of the United States military. The American Ambassador to Chile was deeply embarrassed and asked Washington why he had been kept ignorant of the project. The problem was discussed in the highest levels of the United States government, and the entire project was canceled.

Irving Louis Horowitz has written a careful account of the entire Camelot affair.[15] He has examined the role of the many government officials and researchers who staked so much on the $6 million multicountry study. On the basis of extensive interviews with the social scientists, he was able to present their views about the project, its goals, strengths, and weaknesses. It is apparent that these men defined Project Camelot as a crucial opportunity to engage in a most important comparative research endeavor. They never disguised the source of the financial support. The researchers did not feel that they were naïve about the purposes of the United States Army. Yet many felt that the Army had to be educated to the realities of the current world. The social scientists worked toward the adoption of enlightened policies, and they felt that Department of Defense sponsorship would in no way limit or inhibit their freedom of research.

On the other hand, most of the critics of the project, among whom I count myself, condemn its designers for simply assuming that the United States military has a legitimate role in dealing with social problems of other countries, for asserting that this country's foreign policy was a major factor in determining the site(s) of research, and for implying that internal war is always the greatest threat to a population's well-being. Nowhere in the documents was there a consideration of alternative views or hypotheses.

The Camelot researchers, in addition, ignored some painful realities of contemporary international relations. Camelot's director, Rex Hopper, and his associates naïvely underestimated the amount of suspicion generated by the United States military in 1965. Few Latin Americans active in national life had forgotten the United States backed invasion of Guatemala in 1954 or of Cuba in 1961, or our military intervention in the Dominican Republic just a few weeks after the project became known in Chile. No Chilean social scientist could cooperate with a research endeavor so obviously tainted by United States military sponsorship and interests. The planners of Camelot had condemned themselves by their willingness to integrate Army needs into their project's design.

Indeed, with the deepening involvement of the C.I.A. and the Department of Defense in overseas activities during the last two decades, the credentials of all social science investigators have become increasingly suspect. We know, for example, that the Camelot controversy immediately resulted in the paralysis of several other projects in Chile, studies that had been carefully formulated by respected and experienced researchers who had no connection with military or intelligence agencies. Other research projects and investigators have met with intense suspicion in other parts of Latin America, Asia, and Africa.[16]

Nuttini had failed to gain acceptance in spite of his Chilean background, his statements about the significance of the project, and his offer to include local social scientists in the research. The project statement clearly and openly spoke of supporting the mission of the American military. Its scholarly relevance was defined by the Chileans as a mere cover for espionage. Nuttini was immediately proclaimed a dangerous "spy" who could bring harm to the social science community and to the country as a whole.

An astute researcher must recognize the variety of labels to which he is vulnerable. The field worker in another country loses any chance of doing research if he or his project is identified with his own country's military and intelligence agencies. I shall return to this central issue in Chapter IV. Here it is crucial to reemphasize how significant sponsorship and the nature of the project are in the ability to win even initial acceptance.[17]

## Summary Discussion

While it is difficult to specify precisely the first crucial steps in the field work process, the above discussion does serve to alert us to some of its major highlights. In all cases, the investigator set out with a general idea of the types of questions with which he was concerned. What is the nature of social relations in a slum community in a large city in the United States? What is the life style of underemployed black workers? To what variety of role definitions do Chilean students adhere? What is the social structure of a small, isolated community in North India? What are the dimensions of conflict and strain in a society characterized by apartheid? What is the nature of socialization among army recruits? What factors lead to revolutions in developing countries?

In each case, the investigator knew that his questions and research design would change and develop as he became more intimately familiar with the research setting. The completion of the research design and its implementation awaited the vital step of winning initial acceptance and cooperation from members of the community to be studied. Thus, both Whyte and Liebow developed their entire studies after they had entrenched themselves in community life. My Chilean research was deeply affected by the advice of our new friends. Berreman's project was determined by the amount of openness shown by the high-caste villagers.[18]

The initial stages of the research adventure also reveal how crucial it is that the researcher develop a project that is appropriate to the setting. He must be able to explain satisfactorily what he is about to those whose cooperation he seeks. From their perspective, it may matter little how sophisticated his research design is or how significant the problem. If they feel his queries are inappropriate or, indeed, dangerous to their well-being, he can expect hostility and rejection.

Project Camelot is a prime example of this problem. Many sophisticated social scientists were associated with its formation. They hoped to ascertain answers to the complex issues of social upheaval and believed that the collection of data from many countries would make an invaluable contribution. After its demise, its supporters continued to define Camelot as an impressive intellectual undertaking. William Goode wrote that it was the most important social science effort of the decade.[19] Robert Boguslaw charged the critics with ignorance and personal pique.[20] In Chile, Camelot was simply defined as a dangerous and insulting venture. In the United States eminent social scientists seriously questioned the scholarly value of the entire project.[21]

Beyond the very nature of the project, the initial success of a researcher and his work also depends upon his ability to establish personal rapport with informants and respondents. Herbert J. Gans, a well-known and skilled field worker, has written about this challenge from the perspective of the researcher, and he sensitively explores the extent of personal anxiety that the investigator experiences during the early stages of his work.[22] The social scientist has usually expended a great deal of time and energy in planning his project. But the moment of truth occurs when he meets his first informants. Will they accept him? Will they find him unattractive or too threatening?

Gans sees himself as a reserved and quiet person. He suffers from the fear that others will reject his overtures even, he says, after the research has been successfully begun. Yet he also pictures himself as someone with an "honest face" and a nonthreatening manner. Informants seem to sense his enthusiastic commitment to his work, he believes, and usually react with a willingness to contribute to his efforts. This combination of characteristics may have enabled Gans to win the cooperation of low-income Italians in the Boston West End, middle-class homeowners in Levittown, and most recently, communications workers and executives.

Daniels, on the other hand, has a distinctly different bearing. She is far more forceful and imposing. When studying the military, she did not trouble, at first, to disguise her condescending attitude. The officers, she relates, obviously saw her as a dominating and threatening figure. She had initially made her motivations all too clear. From her perspective the military officers were part of a bureaucratic organization and their assisting her was simply a part of their role obligations. Meeting her professional needs was something about which they had little choice, she thought. The reality was all too different. Daniels was required to modify her bearing and the outward display of her motivations for she had no real power to enforce her definition of the situation. Only as she became more sensitive to them, were the officers willing to accept her. Daniels faced hostility until she responded to the officers' expectations. There was an implicit agreement between her and the officers on the nature of the bargain. She had to show deference and respect in return for their cooperation.

This poses the fundamental dilemma of early field work encounters. All of the investigators discussed above sought the most effective way to win the cooperation of local people. Each field worker quickly learned that suspicion had to be overcome. To achieve this, the field workers promised, implicitly or explicitly, that their work would be beneficial to those under study, that no harm would come from the researcher's presence. Often, the field worker promised far too much. Frequently, at the conclusion of a study, both respondents and field workers pay a heavy price for this often conscious manipulation, as I will make clear in Chapter IV.

There is another pertinent and fascinating area that has yet to be adequately explored by field workers. What do *respondents* see and feel when they interact with the researcher? Would all respondents tell the same story? Do they find Gans a sympathetic and sensitive listener? Is Daniels really so imposing? Did the officers accept her change in personality as "real?"

What of the Indian villagers studied by Berreman? How many were actually convinced by his appeal to their new importance in national and international life?

I have always wondered how the Chilean students viewed Penina and me in our first encounters. How accurate is the image that we conjure up about our efforts in another language? Did others help me because they admired my courage, venture-some spirit, and sincerity of purpose? Or did they, rather, reach out a hand to a pitiful traveler to their country? I felt comfortable with the warmth of Chilean hospitality and de-lighted by the quickly formed friendships. Yet I also knew that my friends were also my constant informants. I desperately needed them. How did they feel about the duality of our rela-tionship? Liebow perceptively asks what his black informants saw when a group gathered with him around a table. What did the Chileans see when we sat in the student cafeteria drinking *café con leche*?

There are as yet no clear answers to these puzzling ques-tions. I know of very few instances in which informants or respondents have been given the opportunity to append their impression of the investigator on the research report. Were they encouraged to do so, we would have a much fuller picture of the early stages of the field work adventure. Respondents normally make their views known only in those situations in which the researcher has failed to win their cooperation, as exemplified by Project Camelot, or when the research report raises the ire of offended subjects, as I will discuss later. The image of the investigator is then blurred by the clouds of hos-tility that real or alleged transgressions have created.

Readers of research reports and future generations of stu-dents would directly benefit were greater effort made to secure respondent reactions in less emotionally charged situations. Neophyte field workers are usually advised by their more experienced supervisors or colleagues. They are rarely exposed to the observations and sensitivities of subjects until they have stumbled through the many practical and ethical pitfalls of the first contacts. Seeing ourselves as others do would be an invalu-able aid in planning future field work,[23] or perhaps, as we shall see later, in deciding that certain kinds of research should not be pursued at all.

## NOTES

1. William Foote Whyte, Appendix: "On the Evolution of Street Corner Society," *Street Corner Society* (Chicago: University of Chicago Press, 1955), pp. 279–358, paperback ed.

2. For a useful and highly readable account of the development of sociological research and thought, see John Madge, *The Origins of Scientific Sociology* (New York: Free Press, 1962). Whyte's work and its relationship to previous research is discussed in detail.

3. There are two other particularly pertinent studies in which the participant observer discusses in detail his problems of establishing an acceptable identity. In one, Ulf Hannerz describes the challenge of explaining who he is and what he wants to black residents of a Washington, D.C. ghetto. Ulf Hannerz, *Soulside: Inquiries into Ghetto Culture and Community* (New York: Columbia University Press, 1969). Herbert J. Gans' problems in establishing an identity in a suburban community were somewhat different; he owned a home in the community and played a variety of research roles. For an important discussion, see Herbert J. Gans, *The Levittowners* (New York: Pantheon, 1967), pp. 435–451. Gans summarizes his various encounters using participant observation in his "The Participant-Observer as a Human Being: Observations on the Personal Aspects of Field Work," in Howard S. Becker, *et al.* (eds.), *Institutions and the Person* (Chicago: Aldine, 1968), pp. 300–317.

4. Elliot Liebow, Appendix: "A Field Experience in Retrospect," *Tally's Corner* (Boston: Little, Brown, 1967), pp. 232–256.

5. The literature on participant observation is extensive. A useful collection that includes a reprint of Liebow's discussion is Glenn Jacobs (ed.), *The Participant Observer* (New York: Braziller, 1970).

6. Frank Bonilla and Myron Glazer, Appendix A: "A Note on Methodology. Field Work in a Hostile Environment: A Chapter in the Sociology of Social Research in Chile," *Student Politics in Chile* (New York: Basic Books, 1970), pp. 313–333. For an excellent account of the challenges of comparative research consult Robert E. Ward, Frank Bonilla, *et al.*, *Studying Politics Abroad* (Boston: Little, Brown, 1964).

7. Gerald D. Berreman, *Hindus of the Himalayas* (Berkeley: Univ. of California Press, 1963), p. 2. Originally published by the Univ. of California Press; reprinted by permission of The Regents of the

Univ. of California. The research experience is discussed in his *Behind Many Masks* (Ithaca, N.Y.: The Society for Applied Anthropology, 1962).

8. Personal correspondence between Pierre L. van den Berghe and the author dated March 2, 1971. Van den Berghe's field work experiences are reported in his "Research in South Africa: The Story of My Experiences with Tyranny," in Gideon Sjoberg (ed.), *Ethics, Politics and Social Research* (Cambridge, Mass.: Schenkman, 1967), pp. 183–197. Some of his other work on South Africa appears in his *Caneville: The Social Structure of a South Africa Town* (Middletown, Conn.: Wesleyan University Press, 1965); and *Race and Racism* (New York: Wiley, 1967).

9. Arlene Kaplan Daniels, "The Low-Caste Stranger in Social Research," in Sjoberg (ed.), *op. cit.*, pp. 267–296.

10. For a fascinating collection of the field work experiences of women anthropologists, see Peggy Golde (ed.), *Women in the Field* (Chicago: Aldine, 1970).

11. Daniels, *op. cit.*, p. 275.

12. Irving Louis Horowitz, "The Rise and Fall of Project Camelot," in I. L. Horowitz (ed.), *The Rise and Fall of Project Camelot* (Cambridge, Mass.: M.I.T. Press, 1967), pp. 47–48. Reprinted by permission of the MIT Press, Cambridge, Massachusetts. Copyright © 1967 by The Massachusetts Institute of Technology.

13. *Ibid.*, pp. 48–49.

14. *Ibid.*, p. 48.

15. *Ibid.*, pp. 3–44.

16. During 1969, an Argentinian colleague asked me about several North Americans who had invited him to contribute, at an impressive fee, to a volume of essays. He was suspicious about the source of the funds. "We Latin Americans," he explained, "must be very careful about our associations with North American academics." Obviously, little meaningful collaboration can be expected from those who are so wary of our motives. As we have seen, social science research always risks the accusation of interference into private affairs of others. This allegation becomes especially prominent when the research is sponsored by and will be utilized by a foreign government.

17. Whyte recently discussed his research in Peru and described the hierarchy of *unacceptable* sponsorship in Latin America. Grants from the Department of Defense are taboo. *The Agency for International Development* is less risky but is also suspect because of the agency's identification with American foreign policy and its

security clearance requirements. "The last thing the Peruvian professor wants is to have it become known in Peru that he has been certified by the *Department of State* as 'safe' to the interests of the United States!" William Foote Whyte, "The Role of the U.S. Professor in Developing Countries," *American Sociologist*, 4 (February 1969), 19. Whyte believes that funds from the *National Institutes of Health* and the *National Science Foundation* are still relatively acceptable. But I think events in Peru, Chile, and elsewhere, during the last few years, have resulted in suspicion of all United States or United States related local investigators. Any United States government financing raises serious questions. The problem of credibility has become central for American social scientists desiring to work in comparative studies.

18. For an insightful account of how a project is affected by the field worker's early exposure, see Blanche Geer, "First Days in the Field," in Phillip E. Hammond (ed.), *Sociologists at Work* (Garden City, N.Y.: Anchor Books, 1968), pp. 372–398.

19. William Goode, "Communications to the Editor," *American Sociologist*, 1 (November 1966), 255–257. Goode has defended *Camelot* as "intellectually the most significant research project under way during the past decade." He confronted the criticism of "interference" and contended that social research often interferes with local living styles. Goode agreed with the late Rex Hopper, who, as director of *Camelot*, regarded implementation of social reform as the best way to "contain" revolutionary situations. Department of Defense "bayonets and mortars" certainly would not be recommended by sociologists.

Unfortunately, as the Chilean students stressed to me, United States foreign policy is not often made by social scientists. It is devised by government bureaucrats to protect the interests of the United States. Latin Americans doubted that the data collected by Project Camelot would be utilized to further their country's national development.

20. Robert Boguslaw, "Ethics and the Social Scientist," in Horowitz (ed.), *op. cit.*, pp. 107–127. Boguslaw dismissed the issue of sponsorship:

The critical question is not necessarily the source of financial support but rather the nature of the conditions associated with any form of financial support. [p. 113]

Boguslaw's attack on the critics would have been far more compelling had he asked why respected scientists remained silent for so long a time. If the project was so poorly designed and biased in favor of the military's interests, he might have asked, how did the statement escape the scathing criticism of those who were familiar with it? In a frank and telling footnote, for example, Kalman Silvert, a distinguished student of Latin American affairs, who read the original project statement, berated himself for not having spoken up sooner and posed a number of deeply disturbing questions:

It should also be understood that Camelot represents no new departure, that the actors might well have felt no need to consult the academic community concerning the ethics of the matter because so much similar work has already been done and is still being done. A difference in scale is not necessarily a difference in type. In any event, to what formalized academic bodies could the Camelot directors have turned for an advisory opinion on the ethics of their undertaking? How many scholars who knew of this widely publicized project actually wrote to SORO questioning the wisdom and ethics of the matter? ["American Academic Ethics and Social Science Abroad: The Lesson of Project Camelot," *ibid.*, p. 84]

I would observe that the problems raised by the project should have been publicly debated long before the recent incidents and exposures. Few social scientists can plead ignorance, claim total purity, or fail to understand the dilemma of their colleagues who have been soundly condemned for actions that previously won acclaim and attendant rewards.

Boguslaw's impassioned defense and counter-critique are reinforced by Ithiel de Sola Pool's positive assertion that social scientists have a distinct responsibility to provide various government agencies with information upon which to make policy decisions. The Department of Defense has been "humanized," Pool reported, by the efforts of many social scientists who were recruited by former Secretary of Defense McNamara. This change, he stated, is a major accomplishment. If social scientists are so concerned about the functioning and policies of the C.I.A. and F.B.I., don't they have an obligation to put their knowledge and energies at the disposal of these agencies? To refuse to do so, Pool argued, results in decision making by government ideologues whose actions often run counter to the knowledge and values of most academics. See his article, "The Necessity for Social Scientists Doing Research for Government," *ibid.*, p. 269.

Pool is justified in advocating the use of social science data in the formulation of enlightened internal and foreign policy. I would challenge his assumption, however, that accurate information necessarily leads the "government ideologues" he speaks of to adopt enlightened policies. Was it faulty data that, within the last fifteen years, has led to United States intervention in Guatemala, Cuba, the Dominican Republic, and Vietnam?

21. Those critical of the substance of the Camelot proposals are vehement in their denunciation. Marshall Sahlins, an anthropologist, categorically states that those working on *Camelot* should not have defined themselves as social scientists dedicated to basic research:

Every citizen has the right to engage in counterinsurgency research and practice. But in my opinion none of us has leave, as scholar or citizen, to so delude himself and others about the scientific legitimacy and disinterested objectivity of this work. ["The Established Order: Do Not Fold, Spindle, or Mutilate," *ibid.*, p. 78].

Horowitz went even further and raised the specter of a captive discipline. He maintained that social scientists have, at times, consciously accepted the perspective of one group to the neglect of other equally legitimate interests:

It is important that scholars be willing to risk something of their reputations in helping to resolve major world social problems. But it is no less important that in the process of addressing their attention to major international problems the autonomous character of the social science disciplines, their own criteria of worthwhile scholarship, not be abandoned. It is my opinion that the ambiguity, asymmetry, and eclecticism of the fragmented and programmatic nature of even the most advanced documents circulated by Project Camelot lost sight of this "autonomous" social science character in the pursuit of the larger demands of society. ["The Rise and Fall of Project Camelot," *ibid.*, p. 32].

22. Gans, "The Participant-Observer as a Human Being: Observations on the Personal Aspects of Field Work," in Becker, *et al.* (eds.), *op. cit.*

23. Until we have these accounts, we can refer to the stinging description of social scientists at work in the novel by Alison Lurie, *Imaginary Friends* (New York: Coward-McCann, 1967). For a fascinating fictionalized account by a social scientist, see Elenore Smith Bowen, *Return to Laughter* (New York: Harper & Row, 1954).

# CHAPTER II

# (A)

# learning one's way around

Gaining acceptance is a critical step in the research process—some investigators achieve it within a few days of their arrival at the research location, while others must wait several months. In either case, the early period of residence also provides the researcher with the opportunity to understand local conditions. Insight gathered during this period contributes to developing or modifying the research design. It can alert the investigator to the reality of his research goals and to the possibility of his completing his work, given available time and resources. It can also sensitize him to the many pitfalls he must face as he continues in the research effort.

This chapter will focus on the various factors inherent in adapting to the research environment and will be particularly concerned with a major tension in the field worker's role. He is constantly challenged by the tendency to become overly involved in the lives of some of those he hopes to study. He must continually guard against the danger of overidentification or what anthropologists call "going native,"[1]—where he forgets his primary goal is to collect systematic data from a social scientist perspective—and he must remember that he has special interests and requirements.[2]

Field workers employing the techniques of participant observation are particularly susceptible to the tendency of oversubmersion in group life. The lines between their own roles and permissible actions can readily become blurred by the demands of group members or by their own desire to be genuine participants. The researcher's loss of control of the direction of his actions and his lessened ability to observe can be the crucial negative consequences of such overinvolvement.

Whether he is a participant observer, an interviewer, or the distributor of the more impersonal questionnaire, the field worker's own perspectives may lure him into a second pitfall. He may, knowingly or unknowingly, act out a previously held or newly developed bias toward a particular group or viewpoint. Thus, his questions may be inadvertently phrased to insure certain responses or his observations may become limited in order to support those results with which he feels most comfortable. This tendency is often exposed and corrected if the investigator discusses his impressions with knowledgeable informants or sensitive colleagues.

Finally, tension in the field worker's role may be expressed by his personal reactions to the very social system that he is studying. Poverty, racial discrimination, and legal injustice often weigh heavily on the investigator. As he experiences these factors firsthand, he may find himself unable to respond in the manner suggested by textbook recipes of appropriate field work behavior. He may feel compelled to take a public stand rather than to maintain the stance of neutrality, which most investigators consider the appropriate tone for presentation. Here the strength of his commitment to the importance of scholarship and to the role that social scientists traditionally play in social problems research is most seriously questioned.

As he faces the challenges posed by overidentification, biased observations, and his reactions to social injustice, the' researcher draws on a variety of people to support him through the field work effort. Consultants, associates, informants, and others play crucial parts. The research adventure is replete with examples in which the field worker reaches out and garners emotional and intellectual sustenance from many whose participation is often crucial to the very survival of the entire investigation.[3]

## CORNERVILLE

WHEREIN WHYTE MOVES TO CORNERVILLE, LEARNS TO AVOID
ROMANTIC OR FINANCIAL ENTANGLEMENTS, BUT SUCCUMBS
TO THE DEMAND THAT HE ENGAGE IN ILLEGAL BEHAVIOR
AND LEARNS THE PRICE OF OVERINVOLVEMENT.

The field worker is a person with a clear purpose—he seeks acceptance into a community in order to study it. Toward that end he must remain ever conscious that his actions should facilitate his movement in that direction. This can best be achieved if the researcher is sensitive to pressures from others or from within himself to become involved when his scholarly judgment cautions against it. Respondents, genuinely accepting the researcher, may often forget that he is not a full participant and expect him to act as any other member. It is the researcher's responsibility to set limits on his own behavior by subtle or overt reminders that he plays a different and special role. Neglecting this caution may result in severe penalties that may endanger the entire research project.

After his successful first encounter with Doc, William Foote Whyte decided that he had to find a place to live in Cornerville.[4] To become familiar with and to participate in the life of the community required time. His efforts could certainly not be confined to a nine to five schedule. Rather, he would have to spend long hours talking on street corners to people who kept no formal hours. He realized that his room at Harvard was simply too comfortable. Whyte sensed that he often preferred to stay there and read instead of visiting the still strange and distant community. His only alternative was to move to Cornerville, and, after searching about, he found a comfortable room with the Martino family.

As Whyte began to make his way around the community, he grasped the important lesson that much could be learned by simply listening. Asking questions, at times, served to silence others. During their first outing, Doc escorted Whyte to an apartment where gambling was going on. Doc introduced Whyte as his good friend, and, when Whyte left the room momentarily, reassured the others that the newcomer certainly wasn't a government agent. Later in the evening, one of the men went into graphic detail in describing the organized rackets. After listening intently, Whyte inquired whether all the police had been paid off. This most untactful query stunned the speaker. The subject was immediately dropped. Doc later coached Whyte about the importance of listening. This was one of many times where Doc acted as guide and teacher.

Beyond learning that his research role required a judicious use of questions, Whyte sensed how careful he would have to be in his relationships with local women. Custom prevented casual friendships. He noted that visiting a girl's home was considered proof of serious intention. While he found many of the women very attractive, he realized that his work could ill afford such an involvement, and he was scrupulously careful.

Whyte also treaded lightly when it came to matters of money. He was in no way hard-pressed for funds and could afford to treat or lend. While this was expected between friends in Cornerville, he knew that such actions might result in others feeling indebted to him. Such obligations could put a strain on their relationship. He certainly did not want anyone consciously avoiding him because of an unpaid loan.

All caution deserted Whyte, however, when he decided to broaden his study by shifting his focus from the street-corner gangs to the political life of the community. He enlisted in the organization supporting one of the local politicians. Assuming the task of recording secretary, he was able to take almost verbatim minutes of the meetings. He felt that his efforts were rewarded by his growing insight into local conditions. On election day, however, he was swept up into a series of events that transformed him from a participant observer to a non-observing participant.

Whyte had been pressured into voting several times as he toured the districts. His last vote occurred in his own district, and, before entering the polling place, he voiced fear that he would be recognized as having voted earlier in the day. He was assured that the poll personnel had changed and that, in any case, he would be voting in someone else's name. He again expressed anxiety for he was posing as a man twenty years his senior and six inches shorter. Whyte almost made it through the voting process but was challenged just as he was about to deposit his ballot. In his fear upon being confronted, he even forgot his assumed name and knew he was trapped. He imagined the headlines in the city newspapers and the damage his arrest would do to his study, his future, and to his university. He was saved from exposure solely because the poll warden was supporting his candidate and covered his blunders.

This experience deeply affected Whyte. He had carelessly risked everything by his actions. In his own report, Whyte emphasized that the researcher cannot afford to forget his primary purpose or pretend that he lacks a sense of proper behavior. Whyte's own middle-class background had instilled in him a deep sense of acceptable political involvement. Yet, he had rejected both his professional responsibilities and personal proclivities. Whyte argued that the investigator must have a clear image of his own role and must strive to maintain it if he is to keep his self-respect. His voting activities had ignored several major precepts of field research; he had abandoned the role of researcher and lost sight of his original goals.

Whyte's traumatic experience in the voting hall mirrors the emotional buffeting to which the field worker is often exposed. Months of careful planning can be destroyed by one injudicious act. The researcher repeatedly learns how exposed he is when he is mistaken in his judgment. The fear that Whyte must have experienced is difficult to record.

Whyte's account also portrays how emotionally and physically exhausting the field work adventure can be. The opportunity to escape the pressure and spend some quiet moments is absolutely essential. Whyte describes how important his room in the Martino home became. He was treated like a member of the family and particularly relished the Sunday afternoon dinner. The easy conversation, abundant food, and good wine offered a welcome reprieve from the hectic week's schedule. Whyte joined in as a full participant, forgot about taking notes, and felt the light gaiety dispel his weariness. A long nap was the final ingredient in the essential diversion.

The field worker who lives among those he is studying needs such outlets if he is to keep a sense of balance. Researchers are frequently exhausted part way through their experience and dislike their work at its conclusion. A crucial aspect of learning one's way around is finding means by which to escape the pressures of constantly being on the job. Whyte's home with the Martino family and his ability to leave Cornerville and visit his friends in Cambridge were essential outlets.

## TALLY'S CORNER

WHEREIN LIEBOW CONFRONTS THE COMPLEX DEMANDS MADE
ON THE PARTICIPANT OBSERVER YET MAINTAINS HIS
COMMITMENT TO BOTH INVOLVEMENT AND DETACHMENT
BY A SELF-CONSCIOUS AWARENESS OF HIS OWN GOALS AND
A CAREFUL USE OF AN OUTSIDE CONSULTANT.

Whyte's experience with illegal voting is a painful example of the difficulty in maintaining the necessary distinction between controlled involvement and blind participation. For in order to understand community life, the researcher must take part. Participation is both unavoidable and beneficial even though risky. The involved field worker can experience the subtleties of interaction that remain simply inexplicable to the outsider.

During his first days on Tally's Corner Elliot Liebow had become deeply embroiled in Lonny's legal problems.[5] His actions were a natural outcome of their growing friendship and increased the confidence and good will of the men Liebow wanted to study. Similarly, he dressed informally like them, noticed a change in his speech patterns when he was with them, placed bets on the numbers, and lent money as others did. In these ways he tried to reduce his position as an outsider and simultaneously gain empathic insight into the men's lives.

Yet Liebow, like Whyte, was cognizant of the special nature of his role. Liebow carefully avoided more personal forms of gambling such as craps or cards, which he felt could compromise his relationship with the men. He was also scrupulous in preventing any suspicion of intimate contact with local women.[6] His goal was to become as fully absorbed into the men's world as possible, to see and feel it as they did, and yet, to guard against submersion and lack of awareness of important events and attitudes. His constant discussions with Hylan Lewis, the project director, were an important source of his sensitivity to the continuing demands of his new role.

A consultant can play an important part in assisting the field worker to reflect on his experiences and the direction his work is taking. Often, as he articulates what he has seen and how he has acted in particular situations, the researcher gains important insight into patterns of attitudes and behavior of those he is observing. The consultant with a lively curiosity can also serve as a source of constant questions about the researcher's own reactions. He can alert the field worker to actions that he is beginning to take for granted and can encourage him to pursue fruitful areas of further inquiry.

Since the consultant is not directly involved in the day-to-day challenges of field work, he is in a particularly good position to help the researcher adapt to the ever-present dangers of over-identification and overinvolvement that can readily narrow the range of his observations.[7] According to Liebow, Lewis was also extremely important in assuring him that his work was moving in the right direction. It is easy for the participant observer to lose confidence in the material he is collecting. He needs someone to encourage him, to help him dissect his data, and to support his feeling that he will eventually be able to put all that he has observed into a coherent whole.

Both Whyte's and Liebow's experiences indicate the great demands made on the participant observer:

The requirements of participant observation are rigorous. What we have said is tantamount to saying that the participant observer must remain a scientist with the insights of a Shakespearean dramatist. No one can expect perfection in such a demanding role, but one can expect researchers to be aware of the professional ideals surrounding it and to guide their work as closely as possible by these ideals.[8]

## INDIA

WHEREIN BERREMAN SUFFERS THE LOSS OF
HIS TRANSLATOR AND DISCOVERS HOW SHARMA'S RELIGIOUS BELIEFS
HAD PLACED BLINDERS ON HIS SCHOLARLY CONVICTIONS AND HAD
BIASED BERREMAN'S UNDERSTANDING OF VILLAGE LIFE.

The researcher intent on understanding community life must avoid distorting his own observations by overinvolvement, by his preconceived images, or by his identification with certain patterns of behavior. Gerald D. Berreman's experiences clearly reveal that the field worker must not only be sensitive to these tendencies in himself but also in his co-workers.

Berreman's impassioned speech described in Chapter I, which led to his initial acceptance by many of the villagers, preceded a series of further challenges to his research effort.[9] Throughout his stay in India, Berreman constantly worried about the health of his family, the petty problems imposed by government bureaucrats, and the suspicions of the villagers. His most pressing difficulty, however, was the illness of his young assistant Sharma, which deeply affected Berreman's morale since his knowledge of the language was not sufficiently advanced to permit him to interview the villagers alone. How could he gather data on community life without the indispensable services of his assistant and translator?

Unwilling to spend a long period of time searching for a new assistant, Berreman hired the first promising applicant. Mohammed was older than Sharma, a Muslim rather than a high-caste Hindu, and far less experienced as a researcher. Berreman's new assistant, however, was less threatening as a sexual rival to the local males because of his age and more readily achieved the cooperation of the low-caste villagers because of his religion. Berreman quickly realized that Mohammed's strength and weakness as an assistant were directly in contrast to Sharma's. Perhaps of most importance, Mohammed had little personal involvement in the data, while Sharma was very much concerned that Berreman have a positive view of Indian village life. Berreman now realized that Sharma had been engaged in subtle manipulation of the information. Sharma's translations had been directed toward allowing the high-caste Hindus to manage the type of impressions that the young field worker was receiving. Berreman also began to observe how the villagers carefully controlled what the outsiders were allowed to know about village life. Thus, because Sharma neither ate meat nor drank liquor, the villagers scrupulously avoided doing this in front of him. However, when the villagers learned that Berreman and Mohammed had no such religious beliefs, they revealed that these practices existed and encouraged the researchers' participation in them. With the help of his new translator Berreman was beginning to break through into the more sensitive areas of village life.

Berreman's relationships with Sharma and Mohammed thus indicate yet another complication that challenges the field worker. Barriers of language may prevent direct access to respondents. Information may first pass through a translator to the researcher. This provides a distinct possibility of bias, which the field worker may find difficult to control.[10] It also establishes another factor of dependency that increases the investigator's already high level of anxiety. On the other hand, Mohammed's background and demeanor not only put many of the villagers at ease but also contributed to Berreman's sense of confidence that he was capable of completing the project. A co-worker may thus become a prime source of support.

Berreman confronted a wide array of challenges throughout his field work, and he recently noted that a number of important personal relationships and decisions sustained him during his residence in Sirkanda:

I derived great satisfaction from my friendship with a few villagers, notably the blacksmith. That is a friendship which has endured and was still strong a decade later. At the risk of sounding oversentimental, I can say that there are few friends who have meant more to me than he. The school teacher was an equally close friend. If it had not been for these two men, my life in the village would have been much more difficult, much more bleak, and no doubt my understanding of the village would have been less. I was actually closer to them than to my assistants in terms of friendship—perhaps because of the absence of the employer-employee relationship which inevitably affected the latter relationship.[11]

Berreman also needed time to get away from the village, to reestablish his identity with people with whom he could fully relax, and to restore his belief that he could actually complete the project. He reveals the importance of family and his own drive to succeed:

I cannot imagine what it would have been like without my wife and small daughter there, or without the regular periods in town. No doubt under either or both of those circumstances it would have been a very different experience.

As it was, I could always escape the loneliness and stress of life among people who never regarded me as one of them and with whom there were always blocks in communication based both on language and on deep-seated cultural differences. I welcomed the opportunity to lose myself occasionally in familiar surroundings very different from those in the village—my home in town, my family, an occasional American movie, an American novel, the company of resident or itinerant Americans in urban areas of the region. On the other hand, I cannot imagine that the research could have been successful if I had not been continuously resident in the village much of the time—both for the opportunities it afforded for observing and entering into life in the village, and for the special identity as "resident" that it gave me in villagers' eyes.

I suppose, in sum, that what kept me going was friendly support (family, friends, assistants), the possibility of escape (solitude, novels, town), and the satisfaction of succeeding in the research enterprise. The first two would have seemed hollow without the third.

In moments of great frustration my impulse was to read a novel, take a hike in the countryside by myself, or even to go back to my town environment. These escapes were crucial. However, I forced myself (and sometimes the forcing was palpable) to walk through the village or the agricultural areas (when work was going on there) twice a day (morning and evening), whether anything was going on, or whether I wanted to, or not—unless there was some special research activity I had to do. That is, I kept myself busy—kept myself interacting with people—on the philosophy that "you can't learn anything if you aren't interacting with people." I consciously exposed myself to interaction as much as I possibly could, and often when I had a strong urge to do otherwise. Much valuable information and many insights came to me in precisely this manner—when least expected.[12]

# (B)

# reacting to social injustice

Field workers often immerse themselves in societies characterized by deeply rooted social inequality. Indeed, this problem and its solution have long captured the imagination and dedication of social scientists, yet the analysis of human suffering places a special burden on researchers. They are constantly plagued by their own feelings of bitterness and anger. Their very scholarly detachment and struggle for objectivity often lead to a profound sense of guilt and impotence. Some field workers hope to strike back through their writings. Others less patient, more action oriented, join the downtrodden and suffer their fate.

## CHILE

WHEREIN PENINA AND I ARE EXPOSED TO THE STARK
REALITY OF CHILEAN POVERTY, SUFFER PANGS OF GUILT,
YET REMAIN DETERMINED TO PURSUE OUR CAREFUL STUDY
OF CHILEAN YOUTH BY DEFINING KNOWLEDGE
AS CONTRIBUTING TO CHILE'S BETTERMENT.

The pulls toward overinvolvement and overidentification, deriving from close and continued interaction with respondents, or the temptation toward selective observation, stemming from personal commitment, also confront the survey researcher resident in a society characterized by naked social injustice. It is not uncommon for the field worker to agonize about the value of his own efforts when children walk about in rags and lofty ideals are pronounced that are little reflected in the daily lives of hundreds of thousands of people. The researcher may begin to ask himself, "What's it all about?" and he may ponder the gains and costs of noninvolvement and a commitment to social research.

The severe problems of adopting to the research setting not only plague the participant observer, but arise for any observer. Penina and I confronted them in our survey study of Chilean youth.[13] The first contacts that we had with Chilean university student leaders had led us to believe that we could proceed with our research plans to interview several hundred students. Yet, we knew how much we still had to learn about the country and the University of Chile, and we decided to spend two or three months making further contacts, traveling about Santiago, and reading the Chilean press. Edmundo Flores, the well-known Mexican economist, whom I had met at Princeton and later in Mexico City, strongly recommended an initial period of getting acquainted with the country. It was too easy, he advised, to begin research and lose sight of the larger national situation. While I had read about Chile, its history, and educational system, I felt this was good advice. We would be more sophisticated interviewers when our firsthand knowledge of university and national reality was greater.

Penina and I traveled, observed, and spent many hours with our friends talking about our own reactions to life in Chile and getting responses to our observations. We lauded the political democracy, the friendly people, the delightful climate, the lovely women, and the enticing wine and pisco brandy. We also expressed shock at the other aspects of Chile—the slums, the garbage pickers, and the beggar children. Even after having read about the slum-dwellers in Santiago and about the burdens of those who inhabit the shacks made of wood, tarpaper, tin, and cardboard, we still had been insufficiently prepared for the effect of personal exposure.

We felt the poverty more keenly in Chile than in Mexico or Peru. There we had been brief visitors and tourists. In Santiago we lived in a lovely house, in an upper middle-class neighborhood that bordered on a *callampa* (slum). This made us a direct part of the extreme poverty and wealth that existed side by side. We found it very difficult to maintain a cool and detached position.

The following is an account from our field diary:

The neighborhood we live in is now being very rapidly developed and is a conglomeration of very expensive, completed homes and those currently being constructed. From our own windows we can see a panorama of the magnificent snow-capped mountains surrounding Santiago; the lovely houses, comparable to very expensive ones in the States; maids forever watering the beautiful gardens; and uniformed governesses escorting children to and from school. Here, as in Mexico, we constantly wonder why, if some have to be "more equal" than others, do they have to be quite so much "more equal"?

Last Wednesday [October 16, 1963] we took a local bus to the end of the line, which is at the very edge of the city. Mountains and wide fields met our view, and, as so very often, we saw a small community of shacks—the famous *callampa*. This was our first real experience with such a *callampa*, and we walked through it, looking at the variety of ragged children and tumbledown dwellings made from scraps of wood, cardboard, and anything else available. We had often wondered whether seeing all these things really had any lasting effect, or whether you went back to your nice house and forgot it all. That afternoon we were sure that, at least for a few hours, we would not be quite the same.

One's reaction is not simple. After the first rude shock, slowly and imperceptibly the memory of these sights creeps into your system. In our own case, it burst forth several days later when we were visited on a cold, rainy, and dreary night by a little boy begging. As we opened the door and saw him standing there shivering, our immediate reaction was to answer "no" to his plea and slam the door in his face. It was like Dickens' Scrooge, who turned aghast when the spirit of Christmas Present showed him the horrible figures of the children of poverty. Fleeing from the immediate sight is much easier than reconciling your feelings.[14]

Our field diary records some of our other initial reactions:

Last Wednesday [October 30, 1963] we visited the Mapocho market. It is a very extensive area near the railroad station. The main things sold are fruits and vegetables.

There was an auction of potatoes going on in the wholesale part and as sacks were sold they were transferred to other containers to be taken away. We noticed several ragged and dirty children hovering around. They were there to collect any fallen potatoes and kept scurrying under the trucks and around the sacks. Some of these "potato snitchers" were with their mothers, who held paper bags and encouraged the children to retrieve the fallen vegetables. Others were alone. It seemed obvious that the children made a regular practice of foraging in this manner. Everyone, workers and bosses, seemed to turn away so as not to interfere in the practice. One worker even handed some potatoes to a woman.

The entire scene—the market, the merchants, the workmen, the women, the resourceful "potato snitchers," the well-dressed tourists, recalled Hogarth's pictures and Dicken's descriptions of nineteenth-century England.[15]

Getting to know our way around had exposed us to the abyss that separated the comfortable upper and middle classes from the *callampa* dwellers who lived on the margins of Chilean national life. We felt the anger that afflicted young radicals who had heard so much rhetoric and had seen so little action from political leaders. We also realized, however, that, painful as it might be, we had come to do a careful study on a representative group of Chilean university youth. We had to maintain good relations with those of divergent political positions and had to understand their view of Chilean reality.

During those early days in Chile my relationship with Penina was the sustaining one. Our home provided a necessary refuge from the myriad of impressions to which we were exposed. It was there that we shared confidences about our sense of exhilaration, the challenges we faced, and our concomitant fears about not being able to complete the study. We retreated there when later events were to show how vulnerable we were to the hostility directed against *yanqui* researchers. Together we could openly talk about the people and things we missed in the United States. It was a release to articulate how attractive it would be to return to the good friends and family so many thousands of miles away, if only for a short time. Penina and I talked about how we needed some perspective on our lives and work in Santiago. Indeed, in retrospect, we know how healthy it is for the field worker when he can actually leave the research setting, as did Whyte, Liebow, and Berreman, even for some short period of rest and revitalization. Lacking the opportunity for respite can seriously affect and hamper the researcher.

## SOUTH AFRICA

WHEREIN VAN DEN BERGHE AGONIZES OVER THE INJUSTICES
INHERENT IN APARTHEID AND STRUGGLES TO MAINTAIN
SOME SENSE OF RESEARCH DETACHMENT.

While the field worker may proceed with his investigation because he believes that his research efforts can contribute to understanding and change, he cannot easily deny that his very presence may give legitimacy to a system he abhors. Thus while he may feel committed to his work, the researcher may remain determined to maintain his own standards of appropriate conduct, rejecting, at whatever the cost, the norms that govern the behavior of his hosts. The risk to the researcher may be more than offset by his own belief that conformity would do irreparable damage to his own values and to his attempt to interact with the oppressed.

The problems that Whyte, Liebow, Berreman, and I had in acclimatizing to the research setting seem to be dwarfed by Pierre L. van den Berghe's experience in the Union of South Africa.[16] His account reveals the tension and horror that he felt as an American social scientist incapable of maintaining a protective sense of detachment.[17] He was intent on doing a study of the nation's apartheid system but was also determined that he would avoid following the restrictive racial policies whenever possible. By way of small symbolic acts of resistance, he refused to be served before nonwhites in business establishments. When filling out official forms that demanded specification of race, he wrote "human." He omitted gaining necessary passes to travel to colored areas and, when accosted by the police, pleaded ignorance of the law. Thus, while he could not actively challenge the government's proscriptions, he was able to circumvent them on a number of occasions.

One incident revealed to him how life-encompassing the regulations were. A colored female colleague, a Muslim of Indian origin, needed a ride home. Van den Berghe offered to drive her. She accepted but very skillfully maneuvered into getting his wife to accompany them. At first he thought that, as a Muslim, she did not want to be seen alone in public with a man. But knowing how emancipated she was, he did not find that "explanation" very convincing. Actually Mrs. Van den Berghe's presence was a necessary protection. Had she not been there, Van den Berghe and his female associate might have been arrested for "immorality." Van den Berghe reports that a policeman was about to stop them but refrained from doing so when he saw the white woman sitting in the back. In South Africa it is a crime for whites and nonwhites of the opposite sex to engage in "immoral or indecent" acts. Under the Immorality Act, this criminal offense is punishable by up to seven years in prison. Simply being together in a car can be interpreted as "intent" to commit such acts.

The taboo they were actively breaking was not riding in the same car together but sitting next to each other on the front seat. Caste etiquette would have demanded that a colored woman sit alone on the back seat. Then her role would have been defined as a servant, and they would have been quite safe:

In this case, the Immorality Act could have been used to punish a breach of caste etiquette, and the policeman's reaction was probably motivated more by anger at the etiquette breach than by a belief that he had a case of immorality on his hands. When he saw my wife in the back, he knew that he could not make the case stick even in a South African court. This is a concrete example of how the simplest forms of interaction across the color line become traumatic and problematic in South Africa, and how the easiest adjustment by far is to become a good racist like all the "normal" people around you.[18]

The knowledge that he was a white man in a racist society plagued Van den Berghe throughout his two-year stay. While those defined as colored suffered the indignities and oppression of legal segregation, white liberals, like the researcher, were constantly torn by feelings of guilt. The simplest amenities became unequally shared privileges. Going to movies, to a swimming pool, or taking a walk was accompanied by the knowledge that nonwhites needed passes in order to enjoy such small pleasures. In addition to guilt, Van den Berghe suffered feelings of anxiety when in the presence of the authorities. His witnessing and hearing tales of torture and interrogation administered by the police left a marked impact on him.

Van den Berghe had lived through the German occupation of Belgium and France. He had experienced the feeling of superiority that came to white men in the Congo. He had suffered the low status of the private in the United States Army. Yet his involvement in South African life affected him much more deeply. He could not protect himself by retreating behind his professional status, for he was immediately and continually exposed to pressures. He was deeply pained by the overt discrimination and violence practiced against nonwhites and he refused the privileges accorded him. Van den Berghe's account is the poignant statement of a social scientist struggling with the tension created by the need to maintain enough social distance to study a society and the desire to lash out immediately and forcefully against a degrading system:

Did I ever want to throw in the towel? No, not really. I had decided to stay there two years, one of which was spent teaching, and I had my research and travels sufficiently mapped out and interrelated to make me stick by them. I was simply too busy and too excited about what I was doing to consider quitting prematurely. Only in the last two or three months did my wife and I start counting the days, and, even then, I kept busy writing. My major fear was that my South African visa, which had to be renewed every three months, would one day not be renewed and that we would be forced to leave before my research had come to fruition. In fact, I was consciously making contingency plans to be able to salvage some of it in case worse came to worse, but

I never considered quitting of my own accord. It is simply not my style not to complete something I have started.[19]

In addition, there were others who shared Van den Berghe's views. He is quite explicit in describing their importance to him as well as the support that his own family provided. Van den Berghe's reaction provides further evidence of the extent to which field workers draw sustenance from others while in the field:

The persons with whom we associate a good many of our best memories in South Africa are the social scentists whose homes in Durban were always wide open to my wife and me and, on Sunday afternoons, were perhaps the live-liest intellectual and political salons in town. These homes were havens of interracial sanity in a mad society, meeting grounds for Liberal party and young African National Con-gress intellectuals, and altogether warm friendly places where we could share our anguish, frustrations, fears, and hopes. In retrospect, the existence of such places in the racist, police-state atmosphere of Durban was a minor mir-acle. These homes were probably the locales of at least 20 percent of my most significant conversations in South Africa. In our own home, we could receive nonwhite guests because we were living in a university cottage and our immediate neighbors happened to be liberals; on one side was a young Canadian couple and on the other side lived one of the fifty-odd Afrikaner members of the Liberal party, literally a one-in-forty-thousand chance. This row of a dozen-or-so red brick cottages where we lived was another one of those rare little sheltered islands where some reason-able facsimile of a human relationship could be maintained across the color bar. Other white liberal friends constantly had to move out of flats because of police raids and neigh-bor complaints about interracial parties. And, of course, the African "locations," being under close police surveillance, were even more difficult as meeting places. My wife was able to take it all with far less emotional strain than I, if only because our screaming infant son was a full-time occupation by himself and because she had the good sense not to read the newspapers and refused to get involved in politics. I occasionally resented her refusal to become emotionally involved, but she doubtlessly helped prevent me from getting involved to the point where I could not have continued my research.

My roles as husband, father, and scholar were sufficiently fulfilling to reduce my political anger and moral anguish down to the level where I could live with them without their seriously impeding my ability to analyze man's seemingly inexhaustible capacity to make life miserable for his fellow-men.[20]

These field work experiences portray the range of challenges confronting the field worker. Whyte and Liebow quickly felt comfortable with the people they were studying and precisely because of this had to maintain some sense of distance in order to observe. Berreman, on the other hand, was constantly anxious about his marginal role. He employed a variety of outlets to cope with his peculiar position in Sirkanda. I felt at ease with fellow students and enjoyed the amenities of Chilean middle-class life. Yet exposure to the marked social injustice eroded this satisfaction and helped me see the many faces of Chilean society. Van den Berghe was repelled by the consequences of the apartheid system. He seemed particularly vulnerable and drew upon friends, family, and his own determination to complete his research.[21]

## Summary Discussion

The demands of the researcher's role necessitate living with tension. This is the price of the research adventure. His adaptation to local conditions requires that he become acutely aware of the pitfalls that may transform him from an observer and analyst to an overly involved, identified participant.

Whyte won acceptance through the good will, confidence, and assistance of Doc, but he quickly learned that a poorly worded query could immediately raise a wall of suspicion. Whyte also came to understand that relationships with local women could compromise his work. Yet he succumbed to the excitement of participation and the desire to belong when he joined a local political party. When he was accepted fully and considered very much a member, his defense against an inappropriate demand was undermined.

Liebow quickly became involved in the serious problems that faced the black men he wanted to study. In the process he won the respect of Lonny, Tally, and others. He also, no doubt, learned much about their attitudes and actions with regard to the courts and police. Liebow believes strongly that the researcher must develop full and giving relationships with those he hopes to study. Acts based on friendship are absolutely appropriate. However, the field worker, according to Liebow, must guard against those demands that can transform him from a researcher to a social worker. Thus Liebow did not become so deeply engrossed as to forget his primary task as a researcher. He had frequent conversations with the project director, Hylan Lewis, and was helped to plan his activity and deal with any doubts over his increased involvement. In this way, an outside consultant can play a crucial part in conducting field work.

The problems of detachment and involvement seem to be particularly trying when issues of social justice are present. The researcher's task is to gather reliable data. Whatever his humanitarian impulses or social philosophy, he must try to retain a high concern for the process of collecting evidence. This obviously does not preclude feeling and expressing anger at the human condition. But the careful formulation of research questions and the gathering of data according to justifiable (and replicable) methods are essential components of research. These requirements demand that the social scientist accept the peculiarities of his role. The researchers' experiences described in this chapter reveal the difficulty of this undertaking. Some were exposed to marked social inequality and harrowing human suffering. Whether in South Africa, Chile, India, or the United States, the social scientists had to adapt to and study situations they often yearned to condemn.

To be sure, some social scientists have rejected this limitation. They have tried to play simultaneously the dual roles of researcher and activist.[22] I will discuss them in detail in Chapter IV. In other instances social scientists have rejected their scholarly role outright and have fought to relieve the suffering of the oppressed. For one of the most dramatic instances of this situation we can turn to the life of the Colombian social scientist, priest turned guerrilla fighter, Camilo Torres. He

decided in the mid-1960s that his religious convictions and
social science training demanded that he take a far more active
role in the liberation struggles in his country. He left Bogotá
and joined a guerrilla band in the Colombian hills. Although
he was killed by an army patrol in 1966 and buried in an
unmarked grave, his life continues to serve as an inspiration to
revolutionary youth throughout Latin America. Scholars and
activists continue to collect his writings and to ponder the
meaning of his life.[23]

## NOTES

1. Albert J. Reiss, in discussing his large-scale study of the police,
   provides some fascinating examples of the problem of "going
   native." He describes an instance in which one of his observers,
   playing the role of a plainclothesman, actually threatened a suspect with a night stick. The observer had forgotten his many hours
   of training and had adopted the police role with a "vengeance."
   Another observer, on duty in a police lockup, adopted a measure
   police officers used to humiliate the prisoners. In addition, he gave
   vent to race hatred that even shocked the very officers he was supposed to be studying. Over all, Reiss notes, the observers tended
   to become pro-police. Observers often saw the men as caught up
   in a difficult system. Reiss' entire discussion is important for all
   those concerned with observation and interviewing. Albert J. Reiss,
   Jr., "Stuff and Nonsense About Social Surveys and Observation,"
   in Howard S. Becker, et al. (eds.), Institutions and the Person
   (Chicago: Aldine, 1968), pp. 351–367.

2. This statement, of course, does not preclude the importance and
   desirability of social scientists engaging in social action projects.
   Indeed, many social scientists have successfully combined the twin
   roles of change agent and researcher. See, for example, the collection of essays in Arthur Shostak (ed.), Sociology in Action (Homewood, Ill.: Dorsey, 1966). Also, Allan R. Holmberg, "Changing
   Community Attitudes and Values in Peru: A Case Study in Guided
   Change," in Richard N. Adams, et al., Social Change in Latin
   America Today (New York: Vintage Books, 1960), pp. 63–107. The
   discussion in my chapter obviously focuses on those field workers
   who were committed primarily to the research role. For further
   discussion of this vital issue see Chapter IV of this volume.

3. For a series of useful case studies on the problems of stress, see Frances Henry and Satish Saberwal (eds.), *Stress and Response in Field Work* (New York: Holt, Rinehart and Winston, 1969).

4. William Foote Whyte, Appendix: "On the Evolution of Street Corner Society," *Street Corner Society* (Chicago: University of Chicago Press, 1955), pp. 279–358, paperback ed.

5. Elliot Liebow, Appendix: "A Field Experience in Retrospect," *Tally's Corner* (Boston: Little, Brown, 1967), pp. 232–256.

6. Ulf Hannerz found it necessary to place similar limitations on his own interactions in his study of a black ghetto in Washington, D.C. As a result, women tended to play a smaller role in his description of community life. Hannerz astutely observes that having field workers of both sexes would significantly augment the insights about these areas. Ulf Hannerz, *Soulside: Inquiries into Ghetto Culture and Community* (New York: Columbia University Press, 1969), p. 209.

7. For a discussion of the importance of consultation and supervision, see Reiss, *op. cit.*

8. Severyn T. Bruyn, *The Human Perspective in Sociology* (Englewood Cliffs, N.J.: Prentice-Hall, 1966), p. 253.

9. Gerald D. Berreman, *Behind Many Masks* (Ithaca, N.Y.: The Society for Applied Anthropology, 1962).

10. Herbert J. Gans provides some insightful observations about guarding against bias when the field worker is studying a community in which he is a resident in his *The Levittowners* (New York: Pantheon, 1967), pp. 444–446.

11. One of the other things which sustained me most effectively was the fact that I found the people and the place intrinsically interesting, even fascinating. I really wanted to work there. I emphasize this because, although it may sound trite, it was something I often thought of at the time and since. It is a kind of romantic feeling, I suppose, but I had looked into a number of areas and at many specific villages before I chose a place to work. From the point of view of the research problem I was originally interested in (contrasting an isolated village with one in close contact with the city), there was no necessity to work in a Pahari (mountain) village. Once I had seen Pahari villages, however, although I subsequently visited several plains villages, it was clear to me that I would have little enthusiasm for research in a plains village. For one thing, the Pahari villages were physically very different and,

frankly, attractive. For another, a great deal was known about plains village life; practically nothing had been written on Pahari village life. So when I found two Pahari villages that fit my criteria, I chose them as the site for research with real enthusiasm (I subsequently was able to work at length in only one of them—the remote one, i.e., Sirkanda). When I felt depressed about the progress of the research, as I often did, I got satisfaction simply from the fact that I was deriving unique ethnographic information—and I got great satisfaction from being in the mountains where the terrain is beautiful and interesting. I never tired of simply drinking in the view from the yard of my little house.

Personal correspondence between Gerald D. Berreman and the author dated March 3, 1971.

**12.** *Ibid.*

**13.** Frank Bonilla and Myron Glazer, Appendix A: "A Note on Methodology. Field Work in a Hostile Environment: A Chapter in the Sociology of Social Research in Chile," *Student Politics in Chile* (New York: Basic Books, 1970), pp. 313–333.

**14.** Penina M. Glazer and Myron Glazer, "Field Notes," October 16, 1963, unpublished.

**15.** *Ibid.*, October 30, 1963.

**16.** Pierre L. van den Berghe, "Research in South Africa: The Story of My Experiences with Tyranny," in Gideon Sjoberg (ed.), *Ethics, Politics and Social Research* (Cambridge, Mass.: Schenkman, 1967), pp. 183–197.

**17.** John Dollard's detailed description of his classic research in the American South reveals the differential ability of researchers to adapt to conditions of racial separation and the biases that must be overcome. As a northerner and a committed social scientist, Dollard was deeply critical of the caste system and its costs to the average black. Yet he knew that he had to proceed with extreme caution if he were to study insightfully the nature of race relations in the American South during the 1930s. Dollard became aware how deeply engraved were his northern biases against the South. He was very sensitive to the traps into which they could lead him; he was not there to confirm his convictions. Despite his sympathy for blacks and for all underdogs, his task was to analyze incisively the complex nature of southern race relations. John Dollard, *Caste and Class in a Southern Town* (New Haven, Conn.: Yale University Press, 1937).

18. Personal correspondence between Pierre L. van den Berghe and the author dated March 2, 1971.

19. *Ibid.*

20. *Ibid.*

21. Hortense Powdermaker discusses the problems of working alone in the field and many others in her intriguing book, *Stranger and Friend* (New York: Norton, 1966), pp. 108–114.

22. For an important recent statement, see Henry Etzkowitz and Gerald M. Schaflander, *Ghetto Crisis* (Boston: Little, Brown, 1969).

23. For a sympathetic biography, see German Guzman, *Camilo Torres* (New York: Sheed and Ward, 1969). For a collection of his writings, see John Gerassi, *Revolutionary Priest* (Garden City, N.Y.: Anchor Books, 1971).

# CHAPTER III

## (A)

## peering behind the stage

Erving Goffman[1] and Peter Berger[2] are among the many contemporary social scientists who stress the "unmasking" nature of their discipline. Social science continually delves into backstage areas of social life and often brings to light patterns of social relationships that respondents and others might desire to keep hidden. In this endeavor, Berger writes that the social scientist will often be involved in a debunking activity. He makes public what many prefer to keep private. He cannot respect the sanctity of popular beliefs or actions. His efforts are probing and analytical. As such he is usually an outsider, sympathetic, perhaps, but seldom totally committed or accepted.

This third stage of the field work adventure often involves a fundamental clash between value systems. The researcher is determined to gather information about the lives of those he is studying. His goal is to seek out the most revealing material, dissect it, determine meaningful patterns, generalize about comparable situations, contribute to the accumulation of knowledge within his field, and perhaps advocate social policy that may influence the lives of his subjects. Some members of the group or community under study, on the contrary, may often seek to restrict the researcher's insight, attempt to manage the impressions that he receives of them, and actively resist his efforts to expose those patterns of attitudes and actions that give their lives crucial meaning. The field worker will use every method to break through these subtle or overt walls of resistance. He will attempt to put himself in the most appropriate places in which to observe revealing aspects of group life, purposely seek to establish relationships with those who possess the insights he desires, self-consciously raise topics about which he feels himself still unfamiliar, encourage informants to provide data to which outsiders are normally not privy, and adroitly bargain for information with knowledge he already possesses. Through all of these techniques, the field worker acts on his commitment to free inquiry and to establish the accuracy of his data.[3] He simultaneously often denies his respondents' desire to withhold information and attempts to intrude upon their privacy.

This chapter examines some of the aspects of social life that the field worker studies as well as the types of resistance that he encounters. The dimensions of this resistance can be visualized as points on a continuum ranging from situations in which the researcher confronts *minimal* suspicion, through those instances characterized by periodic but *limited* challenges to the research project, to those experiences in which respondents or others seek to *terminate* the entire investigation.

Our earlier discussion has shown that field workers differ markedly in their ability to establish themselves among those people whom they hope to study. After gaining initial acceptance, some field workers become so well integrated into community life that they have relatively easy access to a wide variety of local institutions. These researchers face little suspicion or resistance to their efforts. Other field workers who have also proven their sincerity but who are more readily distinguished from their informants by some clear cut differences face greater, if nonetheless subtle, forms of resistance as they collect their material. In this situation, informants seldom forget that the field worker is not an actual group member.

There are many other instances in which local residents have continued to harbor doubts about the researcher's motives or goals. Here the field worker must continually parry on-going efforts to restrict his data gathering. While he may seldom be challenged directly, the researcher knows full well that he, too, is under observation. He is involved in a continual tug of war with those who feel endangered by his investigation.

Finally, some field workers may find that their hosts or their spokesmen have taken a firm stand against any further data gathering. The researcher is clearly warned that he must desist or face expulsion. His alternatives are to acquiesce and accept failure or to mount his own counter-offensive by securing the active assistance of friendly groups.


## CORNERVILLE

WHEREIN WHYTE USES HIS FRIENDSHIP WITH DOC
AND THE NORTON STREET GANG TO PROBE INTO THE COMPONENTS
OF GROUP STRUCTURE AND THE BASIS OF SEXUAL ATTITUDES
AND USES HIS CONTACTS IN THE COMMUNITY TO GAIN FASCINATING
INSIGHTS INTO THE WORLD OF THE RACKETEER.

The field worker successfully employing the techniques of participant observation seeks to be an invisible man. He partakes of group activities and is constantly on the alert for important clues about group functioning long after others have ceased to be concerned about the special nature of his role. This presents some danger to the research project, as we have already discussed. Yet it also accrues to the immeasurable advantage of the observer. Group members continually serve as unwitting informants contributing valuable insights. To the participant observer, others are always on stage and subject to his continuing attempt to understand them, the variety of roles they play, and the nature of their interaction with those within and outside of their own groups.

Unlike many researchers, William Foote Whyte was able to spend an extended period of time in the field. He reports that it took him a full eighteen months to decide on his real interests.[4] As he prepared a progress report for his fellowship committee, he became aware of the research pattern he was following. He was concerned with the day-to-day experiences of particular individuals and of the groups of which they were members. He hoped to be able to generalize by studying a sufficient number, though certainly not all, of the twenty thousand people of Cornerville. Whyte also hoped to enrich his observations by studying interpersonal relations over an extended period of time. He was not content to sketch a portrait, but was determined to show the dynamic and ever-changing character of social life in the community.

Whyte was in an excellent position to pursue this goal. He had established himself in Cornerville as a familiar face and could naturally partake in a wide variety of community activities. Where resistance did occur, it could be readily overcome by drawing upon the support of many friends and willing informants. More important, Whyte continued his intensive and sometimes surreptitious observations causing little stir. Whyte's careful cultivation of friends in many areas of Cornerville life provided him with a flexibility shared by few field workers.

One major aspect of Whyte's research focused on the social structure of the Norton Street Gang, a group of local young men in their mid- to late-twenties. Doc had been its leader for many years. Whyte carefully observed how the members treated each other—who looked up to whom, who had earned what degree of respect from the others. He spent long hours with them and, in exhilarating detail, reported how the group structure was acted out and reenforced even by informal sporting activities.

Bowling represented a major form of recreation. Before the final Saturday night bowling of the season, in which individual prize money was at stake, several of the Norton Street men discussed how they thought each of the members of their team would perform. At first, Whyte took little notice of their statements other than that they coincided with his own thinking. Then he began to realize how clearly these predictions reflected the social hierarchy of the group. Now Whyte really became intrigued with the impact of group structure on individual performance. Why hadn't he noticed before that men who were good athletes often performed poorly in situations where they were competing against their friends? Others, who had less natural ability, responded dramatically to the expectations and urging of their teammates. Bowling, like other sports, required confidence and concentration. The feeling that others counted on you, were rooting for you, indeed expected that you would come through, could make all the difference in a dramatic and tension-filled moment. Self-confidence was a key ingredient in performance. This sense of confidence, Whyte observed, was deeply affected by the performer's place in the group structure.

Whyte was delighted with the observation and yet chagrined by his previous blindness to its significance. He had spent many nights bowling with the men and had felt this would build relationships that would enable him to study other interactions. Bowling also provided a needed time simply to relax. He realized how much useful information he had let slip through his fingers. The men had inadvertently provided vivid documentation and contributed to Whyte's growing sense of insight into group functioning and its significance for individual behavior. Whyte had used his friendship with the men to uncover the ubiquitous impact of group structure. Only after he had completed his book would Whyte need to ponder the potential negative influence of his writings on the self-esteem of the low-status members.

These insights did not lull Whyte into a sense of satisfaction with the progress of the research. There was an entire area about which he still knew very little and yet sensed was of extreme importance. Whyte sought to learn about the social structure of racketeering in Cornerville. He spoke to the Norton Street Gang and his other informants and gained insight from their attitude toward the rackets and racketeers. But this information was insufficient. Whyte wanted to win the confidence of someone actually involved. This proved to be a difficult undertaking, and Whyte carefully maneuvered to gain access to the world of the racketeer. He arranged to be at a banquet honoring the entry of the police lieutenant's son into legal practice and there sought out Tony Cataldo, who operated a local gambling joint and was involved in the numbers game. Cataldo was friendly and extended a dinner invitation to Whyte and his new wife. He was even willing to discuss his business problems. This provided excellent insight into the rackets, and Whyte began to feel that his developing friendship would greatly facilitate the research. Two factors, however, intervened. Soon after their meeting, Cataldo's establishment was robbed. Cataldo's economic situation now preoccupied him. In addition, Whyte later realized that Tony had been disappointed by the status returns of their incipient friendship. Whyte had been introduced to Cataldo as a Harvard professor and Tony had obviously hoped to meet some important people through him. Instead, Cataldo found that Whyte only associated with Cornerville residents. Their friendship cooled as Cataldo realized that he could not use Whyte to enhance his own social position.

Although he had failed with his prime informant, Whtye was still determined to probe more deeply into the functioning of the rackets. He was acquainted with Tony's brother, Henry, and began to seek him out. Henry knew a great deal about the rackets, was interested in Whyte's friendship, and informed him about the life of the racketeer. Whyte also secured important insight into the history and contemporary social structure of the Cornerville rackets from Henry and others. In addition, Whyte directly observed the influence of Tony Cataldo on the Cornerville men. Whyte's careful efforts had paid off.

Whyte provides the reader with an enlightening account of the significance and interrelationships between legitimate institutions and illegal activity. He relates the history of the rackets in Cornerville and describes, in vivid detail, the bloody battles that eventually resulted in the organization of these criminal activities. Those gangsters who were too individualistic, who would not compromise, or who were unreliable, were simply eliminated. As with respectable business, the rackets could not survive without a stable pattern of enforced expectations of behavior. The racketeers established close relations with the police and local politicians who protected their activities. The racketeers also moved into legitimate business in order to diversify their holdings. Many were able to provide their children with the respectability that they had sought to attain for themselves.[5]

Whyte's attempt to understand Cornerville life also extended into the area of sexual relations. He pointed out that even these intimate contacts were very much patterned according to group norms of acceptable behavior. As Whyte had learned early in his research, local Italian families carefully regulated their daughters' activities. Visits to the home were immediately interpreted as an indication of a marriage intention. Thus, Whyte observed how young Cornerville men and women tended to meet at street corners for their dates. Parents, of course, harshly criticized this practice but were unable to prevent it.

During his three years in Cornerville, Whyte had innumerable opportunities to talk to his friends about their attitudes toward sex. It was, of course, a favorite topic of conversation. Cornerville men felt that sexual relations at regular intervals were necessary and healthy. Some visited houses of prostitution, but others defined this as unenjoyable and devoid of the pleasure of sexual conquest. It became apparent to Whyte that these young men adhered to a strict code in their relationship with local girls. Virgins were most highly respected and, while most sexually desirable, were morally inaccessible. A young woman's marriageability was greatly influenced by her virginity, and few Cornerville men wished to compromise a "good" girl. More readily available, in terms of the code, were those women who were known to bestow their sexual favors selectively. They were loyal to one man over a period of time and would reject promiscuous relationships. The danger to the young man in these affairs was in becoming attached to his lover. For while these women were ideal sexual companions, they were considered less than ideal marriage partners. Every Cornerville man wanted to marry a virgin.

The young woman in these relationships was also exposed to another danger. Should she become intimate with another young man at the conclusion of the affair, her former lover might publicly boast that he had slept with her first. These threats encouraged liaisons with men outside of the community where the relationships would, almost invariably, prove less compromising to local women. The Cornerville men also often sought female companionship and sexual satisfaction outside of the confines of the local community pressures. Thus illicit sexual activity had the latent function of facilitating inter-community contacts and social mobility.

Whyte's investigation had delved into a wide variety of community relationships. He had come to Cornerville as a stranger and with the help of Doc and other informants had slowly and painstakingly studied many central and sensitive parts of local social life. His initial major assertion had proved well-founded. Slum life was not characterized by social disorganization and anomie. Norms existed that governed the variety of roles the community members played. To isolate them had taken trust, patience, skill, and, indeed, cunning. Whyte had made a major contribution to the understanding of subcultures, and it is apparent that his research is an important forerunner of many contemporary studies both in the United States and elsewhere.[6] Whether Whyte's research had contributed in any substantial way to the people of Cornerville themselves is an entirely different issue, one that I will confront directly in the next chapter.

## TALLY'S CORNER

WHEREIN LIEBOW STUDIES THE LIVES OF HIS BLACK FRIENDS
AND DESCRIBES JUST HOW DEEPLY THEIR VALUE SYSTEM
AND FAMILY AND WORK RELATIONSHIPS
ARE AFFECTED BY THEIR ECONOMIC OPPORTUNITIES.

The material gathered by the conscientious field worker often leads to astute observations that have implications far beyond the confines of the small group under study. Researchers can pinpoint the interconnections of a subculture and the outer society and expose how vulnerable underdogs are to impersonal forces over which they have no control. It is not unknown for the investigator to become a staunch advocate of those who seem unable to speak for themselves. Researchers, then, not only peer behind the action of their subjects' world but also expose a society that benefits from their underprivileged position.

Elliot Liebow is a social scientist whose work reflects a marked similarity in subject matter, methodological approach, and sophistication to Whyte's efforts twenty years earlier. Liebow analyzed the work experience, the aspirations, and the family and friendship relationships of underemployed black workingmen. He spent many hours standing on street corners, sitting in the local carry-out restaurant or in the men's apartments, visiting with their families, or helping them with their various problems. As a trusted companion, he was there during moments of happiness and satisfaction, as well as the inevitable times of frustration and difficulty.

It is quite clear from Liebow's account that occupational and racial differences constituted a barrier between him and the men. Unlike Whyte, he could never become a true participant in the community. His very observability made it easier for others to withhold information. Yet it also seems apparent that Liebow was sufficiently close to the men to gather an abundance of insightful material on Tally and his friends.

Liebow clearly portrays the nature of his relationship in the following description:

Once I was with Richard in his hometown. It was his first
visit in five years. We arrived in the middle of the night and
had to leave before daybreak because Richard was wanted
by the local police. We were in his grandmother's house.
Besides Richard, there were his grandmother, his aunt, and
two unrelated men, both long-time friends of Richard.

The group was discussing the possibility of Richard's
coming home to stay and weighing the probable consequences. In the middle of the discussion, Richard interrupted and nodded at me. "Now Ellix here is white, as you
can see, but he's one of my best friends. Him and me are
real tight. You can say anything you want, right to his face.
He's real nice." "Well," said his Aunt Pearl, "I always did
say there are some nice white people."[7]

Liebow's account describes his determined effort to view the
world from the men's perspective. He was able to observe and
record their intense work frustration, the dangers they felt in
becoming too close to their women and children, and their
need to readjust their personal aspirations to the harsh socioeconomic realities of black American society in the early 1960s.
Liebow does not romanticize their struggle. He is far too
astute, hard-headed, and respectful. He does, however, probe
deeply into the cultural fictions they confronted and, indeed,
created as they attempted to make their way in a social order
that had only erratic need for their services.

Liebow observed how the men continually tasted failure. The
jobs that they were able to secure simply did not pay enough
to support them and their families. They realistically surveyed
their current situation and future opportunities and saw little
on which to build the kind of life valued by middle-class society.
As a result, according to Liebow, they constructed an alternative system of values that accurately reflected their failure in
their work lives. The men magnified the importance of street-
corner relationships. Here escape could be found among others
similarly trapped in the world of menial and poorly paid jobs.
The importance of family life was often underplayed since it
placed responsibilities on the men that few were able to meet.

Liebow focused on the lives of a handful of men and then
sensitively explored some of this nation's deep-rooted social
problems. He exposed the men's defenses as reactions to debili-

tating social forces and analyzed their life style as a reasonable adaptation to stress and deprivation. Liebow rejected the view that certain attitudes are simply passed along from one generation to the next. If continuity in attitudes and behavior is found, he argued, it results when different generations confront similar problem situations. Only a drastic change in these conditions of lower-class black life, Liebow believes, will affect family and work attitudes and behavior. As long as wage rates preclude supporting a family, many black men will be frustrated, incompetent, and rejected in their kinship relationships. They will continue to build personally unfulfilling ways of reacting to challenges that leave them wanting.

In his concluding chapter, Liebow turned the spotlight on the importance of a more enlightened social policy. Every effort must be made, he argued, toward providing black workingmen with the skills and employment opportunities to support their families. The cycle of poverty must be broken. This can be done if only the proper will is present.

Liebow largely credits blacks with pressuring for the changes that have already been implemented. He warns white middle-class Americans that they will not long be able to enjoy "the good things in their society" unless they become far more responsive to the demands of their oppressed and exploited countrymen.

What is lacking is not know-how and programs but a clarity of purpose, of motive, and of intention. What do we want to do, why do we want to do it, and how much are we willing to pay for it (not so much in money but in terms of basic changes in the class and racist structure of our society) remain largely unanswered questions.[8]

## INDIA

WHEREIN BERREMAN SKILLFULLY GARNERS INFORMATION
ABOUT VILLAGE LIFE FROM BOTH LOW- AND HIGH-CASTE MEMBERS
BY DISCREET PROBING, A NONJUDGING REACTION,
AND A SENSITIVITY TO THE NEED TO VERIFY COLLECTED DATA.

The social scientist may encounter continued resistance to his observations and questioning long after community members come to accept or at least tolerate his presence. The researcher's belief in the legitimacy of his efforts and his ability to delve into sensitive areas while not offending his subjects often help overcome the barriers that stand between the outsider and an understanding of the inner workings of the community. This situation reveals the chronic tension that exists between the ever-probing field worker and his hosts, many of whom may be reluctant to assist him actively, yet hesitant to reject him outright.

Gerald D. Berreman had chosen to study a small, isolated, and closed community. It was characterized by a clearly defined and strongly sanctioned system of social stratification. This system was based upon a mutually shared set of rights and obligations. It behooved those who benefited most directly from this exchange to live up to the requirements of their role wherever possible and, where this was not feasible, to make sure to maintain the fiction of their commitment to these standards of behavior. Those at the top of the social hierarchy certainly sought to prevent outsiders from knowing about their transgressions, particularly in sensitive areas. Berreman's problem was that of moving beyond the ideal conception of behavior into the actual areas of conduct. Much of his information would have to come from those who were lower members of the hierarchy. They benefited least from the system of interaction and were often willing to provide the outsider with penetrating insights.

In the analysis of caste behavior, Berreman observed that the high-caste members encouraged some interaction between the lower castes and outsiders. This had important unforeseen positive and negative consequences for the researcher:

Low-caste people are often more relaxed than are those of high caste in the presence of outsiders. Evidently they have little to fear and nothing to lose in terms of status. They are often used by high-caste people, perhaps for this reason, to deal with strangers. This aggravates intercaste tensions, because low-caste people come to know outsiders (the schoolteacher, the village level worker, the anthropologist) better than do the high-caste people. They learn more of the ways of outsiders, become accustomed to being with them, and even acquire habits and ideas from them. The high-caste people fear what may be passing between the local untouchables and the potentially threatening outsider, and dread that they will be "found out," ridiculed, and hence lose status. They therefore try to get rid of outsiders if possible, or keep them away from close contact with the villagers.[9]

The role of the interpreter was central in Berreman's effort to gain covert information. Sharma, the high-caste plains Brahmin, carefully interpreted to enable the villagers to project the most religious orthodox image. The high-caste members attempted to prevent Berreman from seeing that so much of their conduct was shared by the other castes because a lack of differentiation among castes could only reduce their prestige. Mohammed, the Muslim interpreter, had no such vested interest, and he attempted to make the interaction between Berreman and the villagers as direct as possible. Mohammed also put the low-caste villagers at their ease. As a result, they provided the investigators with an abundance of backstage information. For example, Berreman learned that brothers had sexual access to each other's wives and that animal sacrifices occurred in the village.

At the same time, Berreman came to understand that each caste attempted to downgrade the behavior of the others. The investigator, then, had to exercise great caution in accepting the reports of his informants. Only by cross-checking their statements could he learn which people were reliable in regard to what types of information.

Fortunately for Berreman, those in the high castes were not totally consistent in attempting to manage the impressions he received. At times, as in regard to the practice of paying for brides, a custom highly condemned by the plains Brahmins, informants admitted they engaged in this arrangement. Some thought that the investigators already knew this and sought to defend their actions as consistent with their attitude of paying for everything they were given. They condemned dowries as bringing bad luck.

In one important instance, Berreman learned a great deal through a previously uncooperative villager. This man believed that uncomplimentary tales had been told about him by fellow members of his caste. In an effort to tell his side of the story, he informed Berreman of a situation about which the researcher had been previously ignorant.[10]

The significant observation is the extent to which high-caste members revealed information heretofore kept secret in an attempt to protect themselves against actual or perceived intercaste attacks or in an attempt to belittle the standings of their rivals for community leadership. These occasional cracks in the wall of caste solidarity gave the investigators insights that could be verified through further careful questioning. Indeed, this process increased greatly the store of information available to the investigator. According to Berreman, as he learned more yet responded uncritically, his informants felt less threatened by his knowledge and spoke more freely about areas in which he already seemed to be well-versed. This allowed him casually to raise more sensitive issues. Others now more readily perceived him as a person both trustworthy and obviously privy to many of the village's more quietly discussed matters. A few particularly good friends even confided in him as a nonmember of the community with whom their secrets would be safe.

This entire sensitive process is dependent on the ability of the investigating team to tread lightly as they expand their area of insight. They must be responsive to cues about what they may subtly reveal as they seek to utilize a confidence in order to gain further information. At times, even this sensitivity may prove insufficient. Berreman stated that a low-caste informant refused to give him certain insights into village life until Berreman was actually leaving the village. Only as the informant escorted Berreman away would he speak about certain intercaste illicit sexual practices. Had it been revealed that Berreman knew of these events, the powerful individuals involved would have exacted a heavy retribution from the informant. Under certain circumstances, then, fear could control what intercaste loyalty was not sufficient to prevent.

Berreman cogently records the excitement he experienced as a result of his growing sense of understanding the community life:

I can remember very distinctly when, a couple of months after I began to work with Mohammed I suddenly "saw the light at the end of the tunnel"—and that's the way I visualized it. Prior to that, I had been unsure that I would ever learn enough or get a sufficiently coherent picture of the situation I was studying, to ever be able to do anything with it. Then, quite suddenly, I realized that I was beginning to understand these people and how their lives were organized—then I knew that whatever happened I would have learned something worthwhile—that the work would not have been in vain. It was a great relief and a rather exciting feeling. I think it came with the realization that I had achieved remarkably good rapport with the low-caste people, for I remember that it came to my mind that I could focus the study on them if the high castes remained aloof; I realized that there seemed to be few barriers to acquiring information about the low-caste people, or to interacting with them. It was at about the same time that I thought I had a fairly comprehensive picture of the economic organization of the village and of the caste structure. These accomplishments gave me a feeling that the work would in fact succeed—and that was the light at the end of the tunnel.

Prior to that point, I had a lot of data, but the data didn't seem to add up. There were too many inconsistencies, too many gaps, too many contradictions. It was a rather sudden occurrence when the pieces all began to fit together. Somehow, that happened at about the same time that I realized that the missing pieces were likely to be found. It was a combination of feeling that the inconsistencies and apparent lack of pattern were becoming resolved, and feeling that the missing data were obtainable. Closure, which had theretofore seemed so elusive, then seemed to be only a matter of time and hard work. The depression was not derived from the hard work necessitated, but the

anxiety that the hard work might not pay off. The relief—
the light at the end of the tunnel—was not the result of
finishing the work, but realizing it *could be finished*.[11]

Berreman's determination led him to the backstage areas of
village life and helped him expose, among many other things,
the functioning of the caste system. He analyzed the advantages
and disadvantages for the various groups involved. He also
trenchantly observed the resistance to a system that allocated
social rewards so differentially. His statement is applicable to
South Africa, Chile, and to the United States:

What these facts do reveal is that there is more to caste
than its ideal structure. Human beings are involved, and
the effects of the system on the individuals who live in it
must be understood if its functioning in reality is to be
understood. Despite pious statements to the contrary
in India and elsewhere, no group of people has been reported which relishes a life of deprivation and subjection to
other groups. That people submit to depressed status does
not mean that they feel it is justified nor that they would
not like to see it changed, nor, in fact, that they would not
do everything in their power to change it if given the
opportunity. The rationalizations for caste status which are
consistent and convincing to those who benefit from them
or are unaffected by them seem much less so to those whose
deprivation they are expected to justify or explain. Adher-
ence to a religion or a religious principle may not significantly affect attitudes and behavior to which logic would
seem to tie it.[12]

Like the youthful Whyte, Berreman's first major field work
experience proved him an adept and agile investigator. As in
the case of Liebow, Berreman gathered data on the costs of
social inequality. Like both Whyte and Liebow, Berreman
raised no serious questions about the legitimacy of his probing
techniques. For Berreman the major challenge lay in overcoming the villagers' continued resistance. He did not self-
consciously confront the dilemma inherent in befriending others
in order to use them as the vehicle for his recordings and
analysis. Anthropologists and other social scientists have become far more sensitive to this very issue in the last few years.

## THE POTLATCH

WHEREIN HYMAN SUCCEEDS IN OBSERVING A RARE CEREMONY
AND COMES TO QUESTION THE ENTIRE ANTHROPOLOGICAL EXPERIENCE.

A field worker's very ability to probe into the areas that his informants define as most private may cause him to suffer long-felt pangs of guilt. The investigator may come to question the authenticity of field work relationships when he finds himself self-consciously manipulating others for his own ends. Young researchers, particularly, may decide that their attendant anxiety far outweighs the rewards of social science research.

In 1967, Jerry Hyman, a graduate student from the University of Chicago, returned to Taku, in southeastern Alaska, to study the potlatch. Hyman had previously spent a summer on the island and had been invited back by two local friends, David and Sarah, who were giving a potlatch of their own. He quickly learned, however, that the chiefs and influential village leaders opposed his presence at the ceremony. Hyman's hosts, poor and with little influence, had been forced to acquiesce. Hyman, deeply disappointed, implemented a plan to overturn their decision. He first clearly spells out the importance of the potlatch and his reasons for desiring to observe one:

There are two particular ritual systems in the world's ritual repertoire, of consistent, perduring, almost consuming interest to anthropologists. Both initially introduced into the literature by our own anthropological clan founders and culture heroes, the one by Malinowski the other by Boas, they have become the archetypal anthropological rituals. The one is the kula ring of the Trobriand Islands and the other is the potlatch of the American Northwest Coast. Perhaps because of the inevitable personal comparisons (no doubt unflattering) with, as [Clifford] Geertz has put it, "this consummate fieldworker," perhaps because it has, for that reason, become part of our sacred—and hence untouchable—tradition, no one has attempted a second, integrated, systematic study of the Trobriands and the kula.

We are content to genuflect in the direction of the kula without a penetrating reanalysis.

To a lesser extent we have ritualized the potlatch as well. While receiving a great deal more theoretical attention and reanalysis, the potlatch has received not very much more empirical, ethnographic concern. And so while I, like the legions before me, became infected by the potlatch spirit, I was determined—having no flattering reputation to jeopardize—to chance the ethnographic equivalent of Pascal's leap. I wanted to know what had happened to the old potlatch—the ritual, life-crisis cycle of conspicuous consumption, obligations to give and to return, "fighting (for prestige) with property," etc., etc.,—that had, in an earlier time, been associated with totem poles, house fronts, clan feasts, and magic. But I resolved that my own peculiar theoretical infection would be resolved only by my own particular empirical encounter with a real, live potlatch.

I had returned to Taku to study the potlatch on the "invitation" of David and Sarah who were giving a potlatch of their own. During my month's absence, however, the social dynamics of the village had changed. At the instigation of a big chief, either before or just after my return, the village "had decided" to exclude me from the potlatches (i.e., the chief wanted me excluded, enlisted the support of other chiefs and influential leaders and no one else cared enough to oppose them). The "decision" came to me indirectly, of course, through David and Sarah. I would not be invited to the two large potlatches. People were starting to "be against me." I had visions of being expelled. I was a graduate student doing my first piece of field work. Clearly, if I had anything with which to fight I would have to use it now to counter the growing, hardening opposition.

I'm sure I must have begun with David and Sarah. They were relatively poor; they needed money for their own party; I represented, through a "generous" estimation of room and board costs, an income they could now (more than ever) ill-afford to lose. I impressed this upon them. If I needed them, they also needed me. I don't imagine I was particularly merciful in my presentation of such a vital perception, and, if I was, it was likely less as a matter of mercy (I was very fond of them but this was a vital matter as I saw it) than as a posture calculated to achieve the desired effect. I was fairly sure that if I simply laid low, remained at home and inconspicuous, people would "forget" I was there and I would be in no danger of expulsion. My moves with respect to David and Sarah were calculated to assure at least this minimum security.

But I wanted more than that. I had come to study potlatch. I felt I had to see one. I was excluded from the two large "traditional" ones. There was nothing I could do about that. But there was the third party, admittedly (because of its relative humility) treated in the village as something of an afterthought, but no less on that account a real party from the anthropological perspective. And over this party, given by "my own family," I had at least some leverage. I moved calculatedly and cautiously to actualize it. The potential prize was a firsthand look at a potlatch and the attendant academic success. The potential cost was academic and personal failure, expulsion from the village, and return to Chicago as an ethnographic washout.

I began simply asserting in the house, in off-hand, indirect sorts of ways, my acceptance of the already tendered invitation. I would say things like "When our party comes...," "I can't wait to ...," "Will I be sitting with ..." All very indirect and periodic, with intervals calculated to be long enough so that the family would feel unjustified in becoming angry but short enough to keep my continued participation the foregone conclusion I labored to make it seem. I sat at the kitchen table where the family planning took place even though I couldn't understand the half-Tlingit, half-English in which it was discussed. I used one boy, an orphan whom David and Sarah were paid to raise, as a kind of "spy" within the household: he would translate from the Tlingit conversations they may not have wanted me to understand. I kept the pot simmering.

One night they went to a meeting of all the families giving parties. I was, of course, excluded. I went to bed early but I stayed awake. They came home late and went to the kitchen table to talk. I could tell by the tone that things had not gone well. I planned what I would do.

The next morning when I went to breakfast there was a

mortuary-like atmosphere. No one seemed to be talking to me or even looking at me. Finally, Sarah, the strongest of the sisters and in-laws assembled in the house for the party, sat down at the table next to me. "I don't understand it," she said. "How the people are against you, Jerry. I don't understand it. I have never seen anything like it." She explained how poor they were and how relatively weak. She was sorry, she said, and she hoped I would understand, but they couldn't invite me to the party because of what the big shots had said and decided. The crunch had come.

I played it cool. I certainly didn't want them to do anything which would get them into trouble, I said, and if that meant I couldn't go to the party, then I couldn't go. I would just have to talk to them about it. (I was covering myself just in case.) That's what I said. It's not exactly what I meant.

Around mid-morning, I left the house and went down to the grocery store. I ordered a case of soft drinks and asked that they be delivered to David and Sarah's. I paid for it and said nothing more. I knew I didn't have to. David and Sarah would know who had sent the drinks probably before they even arrived at the house. (It was said in the village that a piece of gossip whispered at one end of town would beat you to the other end.) I also knew what the drinks meant. Drinks were the kinds of things kinsmen and only kinsmen were expected to donate to a party. They constitute elements of hospitality at the party and are therefore appropriate only for kinsmen to contribute. Their acceptance of the drinks, a symbol of kinship, was tantamount to the creation of a fictive kinship relationship between us. It was of course possible for them to refuse the gift, but given their financial position and the social strain of refusing, I guessed they wouldn't.

I went to visit a friend while I waited for the social brew I had concocted to take effect. I arrived home just before lunch and walked in as though nothing had happened. I went to my bed and sat down to write a letter. Sarah came over. "Did you send a case of soft drinks?" she asked. I said I did. "Why?" she asked. "Isn't that what kinsmen are supposed to do?" I asked back. "Yes," she said, "it is. Thanks." I told her she was welcome. In fact of course, it was I who was welcome. I had recovered the initiative. I knew what would have to happen. There would have to be at least another kitchen conference. After lunch I left again to let it happen. Sometime in the following couple of days Sarah must have talked to people, because she returned one day to tell me that as her kinsman I would certainly be invited to the party. I knew I was forcing the family to buck village pressure.

I was unprepared for the final blow, however. Two nights before our party David, Sarah, and the others went to a final meeting. I was taken completely aback the next morning (only one day before our party) when Sarah again joined me at the table and repeated our first conversation. The pressure to make her exclude her kinsman must have been overwhelming. I again said that I didn't want to cause trouble, adding this time that it was after all the obligation of a kinsman to help. I was defeated. I again tried to secure assurance of at least a secondhand description. I would have to settle for that. There was nothing to do but retreat gracefully and wait the party out.

We spent the rest of the day preparing the food for the party. Sometime in the late afternoon Sarah and her sister called a kitchen conference. They had miscounted, they said. There was not enough meat. They would need more. Where could they get another deer? Someone suggested a matrilineal cousin who, he knew, had just shot one. One of the boys was dispatched to get the deer. He returned half-an-hour later to announce that the price was $20. The family was flabbergasted. Their matrilineal cousin, a member of the corporate group charged with giving the party, was charging them for what was, after all, his obligation as a kinsman to donate. They had never heard of such behavior. He was a young adult about my age. This is what was becoming of Tlingit culture. David went to speak with him. Much as it rankled, they would offer to replace the deer with the next one they shot. The cousin was adamant. He demanded the $20. The family decided to refuse. They would not pay a kinsman for what was rightfully theirs. Still they were deerless and were therefore about to be seriously embarrassed.

My final chance had come. I waited 'till the whole thing had been settled in the early evening. It was too late for any more village meetings. I told Sarah I knew a teacher who had just come back from a hunting trip with some deer. I volunteered to see if I could get one. I told them to let me know the following morning whether they wanted me to do so. I knew the pressure would mount as the hours passed, and I knew that they knew what my getting a deer for them meant. They were reluctant to search out another deer at the time because they were afraid of the potential embarrassment at having to admit that one of their own kinsmen had refused to help them. A kitchen conference was called.

By morning there was still no decision but desperation began to set in as the time passed. If they wanted the deer at all they would have to act before it was too late to prepare and cook it. They asked me to try to get it. I went to the teacher's house before school started. He did in fact have an extra deer and would be glad to sell it. I bought it for $20 and took it home on the family sled.

The ethical tension had been escalated. Not only had I defined myself as a nuclear kinsman earlier, I had now come through as a kinsman when "real" kinsmen had failed them. I would not of course accept payment; a kinsman did not accept payment for contributing to his own family's potlatch, I told them. They were stuck. At least they had a handle against the community pressure. No one could deny their obligation to invite me.

That night I attended my first and only party. I therefore became, by definition, a Tlingit. I left Taku the same week.[13]

Hyman cannot accept any glib assurances about the appropriateness of his behavior. For him, manipulating the people closest to him in the field raises the most fundamental of ethical dilemmas. Hyman has probed his own motivations. Had he used others to build his own self-esteem as a fledgling anthropologist? Was he primarily concerned with advancement within his own profession and the rewards that only his teachers and peers could provide? Should he now refrain from any other research adventures?

There remains then the fundamental question, by no means answered, whether a person who attempts to be decent and ethical can ever again engage in the encounter we call field work or whether, having once experienced it, it becomes irrevocably, like Masefield's sea, an obsession with ever increasing compulsion.[14]

Hyman has lived through and agonized about one of the fundamental dilemmas of the field work endeavor. There is no escaping the tension he describes. The investigator, whether in Cornerville, Washington, or Sirkanda, will continually bargain for information. When this fails, he not infrequently will use, manipulate, and cajole other people. His prime informants will usually be those with whom he has established the closest relationships. They will often willingly be his accomplices and co-workers. At other times, they will serve as unwitting carriers of personal or community secrets. They will also attempt to withhold certain kinds of information. The field worker can occasionally respect their desire to deny him, but he cannot do this too often and succeed. All researchers must constantly confront the painful dilemma deriving from the use of pressure and manipulation. It is an integral part of their work lives.

Pierre L. van den Berghe, whose experiences in South Africa I discussed earlier, rejects the view that the field worker holds all the trump cards in his dealing with others. On the contrary, Van den Berghe staunchly maintains field workers are often at a great disadvantage and should not recoil when they are successful in gaining entrée and insight:

Hyman implies that the anthropologist is a potent manipulator exploiting unsuspecting and naïve subjects, and taking unfair advantage of his all-powerful conceptual apparatus to bend people to his will. This, I would suggest, is a vastly overrated view of the anthropologist's power and competence. It is true that the anthropologist who directly or indirectly acts as an agent of colonial or imperial interests may thus wield a great deal of vicarious power. That role I regard as peculiarly abhorrent and unethical. But the anthropologist representing simply himself is much more often closer to the bungling fool than to the omniscient and omnipotent manipulator. While in the field, I have felt at least as often the object as the initiator of manipulative acts. Again and again, people in the field have tried to deceive, exploit, and control me for their own selfish ends. The image of the noble savage is still with our profession;

by now, we should know that knaves are about equally represented in all groups. Actually, if any cards are being stacked, it is not on the side of the anthropologist whose conceptual apparatus is far from formidable. It is on the side of the "natives" who know the rules of the game which the anthropologist is trying to discover. Why should the anthropologist feel guilty if he occasionally makes a right move? Anthropologists and "natives" are about equally ethnocentric in assuming that the other party to the field relationship is naïve. I was *never* in a field situation where at least some of my subjects, and indeed nearly all of my informants were not at least as sophisticated about my motivations as vice versa. To assume otherwise is, I think, a piece of arrogance. I would even go so far as saying that the very essence of the anthropologist-informant relationship is a kind of semi-conspiratorial game between two alienated, analytically detached persons testing their perceptions of reality against each other and against the informant's society. Any informant worth his salt is, in the most fundamental sense, a colleague, i.e., a fellow intellectual getting his kicks out of an understanding of the behavior of his fellow men.[15]

The American Anthropological Association has recently taken a different and unequivocable stand on this issue. All anthropologists, the Association argues, must realize the extent of their obligations to those whom they study. There can be no more important relationship to the ethically sensitive researcher. Local people must never be misled or ill-informed about the nature and goals of the research. They have every right to have their identities and sensibilities fully protected. No field worker can make false or ambiguous statements because he wants access to material that would be difficult to obtain were he to make a forthright statement for assistance. The highest value, then, is concern with the well-being of the respondent and not the accumulation of desired data.[16]

This stand puts the Association on record as condemning the use of widespread techniques that involve any modicum of deception. It also raises a myriad of problems that will be ignited in actual field relationships. Any exposure, by a respondent's definition, of any sensitive act, any critical stance that might undermine the authority, prestige, or income of any group could lead to the condemnation of the guilty field worker.

From my perspective, the code is both impractical and undesirable. While making good copy to salve the conscience of legitimately troubled field workers, it can only further cloud the controversy about appropriate behavior in the field. Public allegiance to its standards would create the kind of cultural fictions that Robin Williams has described. Researchers would speak "as if" they adhered to these principles. They and others would know, however, that this is simply not feasible.

Social scientists, including anthropologists, cannot put blinders around their perceptions of the realities in which they work. No such code can protect them from making the painful decisions that afflict the field worker intent on studying the lives of others. However, I believe that the code and others like it can serve a useful purpose. Such codes can alert practitioners to the variety of conflict situations that are inherent in social science research as it is now practiced and can help prevent an easy acceptance of deception. The debate over explicit standards can inform neophyte researchers that, like Jerry Hyman, they will continually make difficult decisions for which they are fully responsible. It can force graduate schools to put more of their energies into raising sensitive issues with their students before sending them out into the field uninitiated and unprepared to stumble through a maze of ethical twists and turns.

In addition, all researchers should be forced to look more honestly and openly into their own motivations for pursuing certain kinds of projects and using certain techniques of data collection. Are we willing to manipulate others because of our prime commitment to what we consider a higher calling? Is it truth and the beauty of knowing that holds our fundamental allegiance? Or, as Hyman asserts, aren't others often exposed for our personal advantage? Isn't it the quest for professional rewards as well as intellectual satisfaction that often propels us? Don't we inappropriately disguise, even from ourselves, our own lust for adventure and fulfillment by proclaiming an unselfish identification with the goddess of science? We have not, as yet, invested sufficient energy in pursuing the answers to these fundamental issues. Thus, when they are raised by others, we feel exposed and, quite justifiably, exceedingly defensive as we shall now learn.

# (B)

# resistance intensified

The social scientist cannot accept uncritically an official statement about an event or a group's rationale for its behavior. If rackets are ubiquitous in spite of moral preaching, as Whyte observed, it is the researcher's task to uncover why this is the case. He tries to unravel the net of relationships that ties the perpetrators to the presumed regulators. Where marked social inequality prevails, the researcher critically explores the complex ideology that espouses the superiority of those on top and the inherent or learned inferiority of those below. Beyond this, the social scientist, as in the cases of Liebow, Berreman, and Hyman, also examines the nature of the performances by those in different statutes.

To succeed in this unmasking action, the researcher will listen to what is being said and left unsaid, to the tone of voice that reveals unexpressed feelings. He will piece together information and try to barter his knowledge for further insights. Most of all, he will be relentless in his pursuit of those who can provide him with the entrée and material that he desires. As a result of his probing the investigator may face *respondent* rejection long after winning initial acceptance. Occasionally, as a natural outcome of his commitment to gather data, the researcher may even move into the more shadowy areas of ethical behavior by disguising himself or his recording equipment in order to secure more accurate information. Because of these actions he may incur the wrath of *public officials* determined to end his project. His own *colleagues* may debate and criticize his methods when he gives respondents no choice in deciding whether or not to coooperate with him.

Charges of deception and betrayal often haunt the field worker when others cast him in the role of villain and attempt to label him as an unwelcome and dangerous stranger, or a subversive and unethical busybody whose actions reflect not his commitment to the highest scholarly values but rather his neglect of the simplest rules of social interaction. The researcher must defend himself and his project in a public confrontation.

## CHILE

WHEREIN PENINA AND I BEGIN TO BELIEVE THAT CONDUCTING
SURVEY RESEARCH IN SANTIAGO IS RELATIVELY SIMPLE,
BUT SOON LEARN JUST HOW VULNERABLE WE ARE TO CHARGES
OF DECEPTION AND SPYING BY PREVIOUSLY FRIENDLY STUDENTS.

When working in a politically tense atmosphere, the researcher and his associates are always susceptible to accusations of spying and betrayal. The accumulation of knowledge can always be interpreted as a threat by a variety of respondents. The field worker may be continually called upon to reestablish his credentials. His national background can be a disadvantage whenever events make all strangers suspect. The line between legitimate social science research and reprehensible spying for a foreign power easily becomes blurred in the accusations of the wary. It often falls to the researcher to prove to respondents that important boundaries do exist between these activities and that his investigation continues to merit confidence. During a period of great stress a few loyal supporters may stand between the project and its total collapse.

Our months of residence in Santiago, discussions with friends and informants, travels throughout Chile, and extensive reading culminated in the preparation of a twenty-four page interview schedule.[17] With the advice of many Chilean friends, Penina and I had focused on a number of major issues. We hoped to uncover information about the students' backgrounds, their reasons for selecting their careers, their own evaluations of their educational experiences, their goals for their professional futures, their willingness to accept positions in urban slums or distant rural areas, and their definition of their political position and of the major problems facing Chile. Our aim was to test some of the critical views in vogue about the lack of professional responsibility and dubious political rationality of Latin American students. The problems inherent in actually doing the interviewing revealed a great deal about many of these issues and about the sensitivity of some respondents to the presence of a North American researcher.

By the time the school year opened in March 1964, we had obtained the services of three Chilean students and professionals to work with us as interviewers. Two of these, Alberto and Gabriela, had helped in drawing up the questions and were to prove essential later in warding off suspicions about the study.

The presidential campaign in Chile had also officially commenced, and a series of dramatic events deeply affected the course of our research efforts. An unexpected defeat in a provincial by-election led to the breakup of the incumbent conservative coalition. The struggle now lay between the center-left Christian Democrats and the far-left Marxist parties, the FRAP (popular front). Intense emotions swept the nation.

In this atmosphere, screaming headlines in early April announced that the Brazilian military had moved to overthrow the legally constituted government of Goulart. Many Chilean students believed the newspaper reports in the leftwing press that the C.I.A. had been involved in the Brazilian upheaval. The students pointed out to us the serious implications of the situation for Chile. Was it not possible and even likely, they argued, that the United States would act similarly were a leftist government to gain power in the September presidential election? American policy in all of Latin America was coming under heavy attack.

The repercussions for us began in the School of History as Penina was interviewing a member of the Communist executive council. He challenged our motives and demanded a copy of the interview schedule so that his colleagues could ascertain the "real" goals of the research. The student believed that our questions had been designed by United States intelligence agents. Responses, he asserted, could be used "to neutralize democratic elements" in the event of future military intervention.

Obviously, his suspicions could have very serious consequences. The Communists were very strong in the School of

History and, if they chose to, could prevent the successful completion of the interviewing. We were deeply concerned and immediately asked Alberto, who was a friend of the Communist student, to explain who we were, what kind of work we were doing, and why we had included political questions. Alberto later reported that he had spoken to the student and had allayed his worst suspicions by stressing that the study had not been devised by American intelligence agencies, but that, on the contrary, Chileans, including himself, had been involved in every stage of its planning and execution.

Other students, however, became increasingly critical of our work. The fate of the project still hung in the balance. Those who were not in political groups seemed most frightened. They asked how I had chosen certain students to interview, why the most radical seemed to be on my list, and what would happen to the information. I showed them the book of random numbers that had been used to draw the sample and stressed that all students had an equal chance of being selected. I retraced the origins of my study and emphasized my position as a graduate student intent on doing a thesis. These explanations convinced most, but a few remained critical of our survey and our intentions.

Even more serious accusations arose simultaneously at the Institute of Science. The students met with us before deciding on their course of action. We tried to allay their fears by appealing to their feeling as scientists. We stressed how difficult it was for science to gain acceptance as a field of study in Chile and how innovators' efforts and goals were often misunderstood. Could they now impugn the motives of someone else attempting to engage in research? To accuse us of espionage, we pleaded, was absurd. At this point, one student indicated the basis of his fear. Although it was claimed that their names were not known and would not appear in the study, he charged that we knew all about him from the number of brothers and sisters he had to where his parents had been born. It would be an easy matter to piece together his identity. In a poignant statement filled with reproach he said, "I helped you and answered your questions, and now you don't know how sorry I am. You have my life in your hands."

What was the cause of such fear? Why had it erupted in a school that was highly unpoliticized and where our interviewing appeared to be progressing so well? It is essential to understand that in Chile there were very few jobs in the field of science. It was very important for a young scientist desiring to do significant research to obtain a graduate fellowship for study abroad. How could they be assured that their support of the left wing, or that their criticism of the incumbent Chilean regime, would not result in their failure to secure a United States visa? Our friends later told us that stories constantly circulated about the type of information that the United States Embassy accumulated. It was certainly not unknown for radical students to be denied entry to study in the United States. In this situation general suspicions of our government's motives had been heightened by fears for their future professional opportunities.

These events were personally painful but intellectually rewarding. They revealed far more than simple verbal responses and contributed a vital dimension to our understanding of Chilean university life, which was corroborated by the survey results. In a few short days a panorama of attitudes and values passed before us. We had been swept up into the realities of national professional and political life.

We had sought to understand how professionally committed science students were. It became readily apparent that many were deeply concerned about their professional futures and extremely anxious about real or perceived threats to their opportunity to pursue graduate studies. Students enrolled in the sciences in Chile had embarked on a risky venture. They could only expect long years of arduous study and a professional life devoid of easy acceptance. Their own professors had warned them of the scarcity of jobs, prestige, and financial rewards. Yet these students had accepted the challenge to innovate because they believed that they could contribute to national development and enhance their personal growth. In this school no ritualists were found, no students simply intent on getting a degree but little concerned with the actual intake and implementation of professional knowledge. All the stereotypes of Latin American students were challenged by them save the one that student respondents in a highly politicized nation with great social and economic problems would define situations in political terms and view North Americans in times of tension as real and direct threats to their own situation.

The attack on our project also taught me a great deal about

myself. I could argue quite legitimately, I think, that no individual student would be hurt by our questions. The interview sheets were to be destroyed. But could I really be sure that my study could not later be used by my country's intelligence and military agencies? It was clear that United States agents were active in almost every part of the world and were particularly interested in Latin America. My concern that *I* had been unjustly accused and my determination to finish the study had made me more insensitive to some of the brutal realities of cold war international politics than I like to think. My investment in time, energy, and self had resulted in my building a rough wall of defensiveness between me and some of my harsher Chilean critics.

I remember meeting one of them at a dinner party shortly after terminating our study at the Institute of Science. I was furious with him and bitterly denounced him when he casually asked how my work was proceeding. My anger, no doubt, expressed how vulnerable I had felt only a short time earlier. But it represented something far more important. "How dare he," I said, "attempt to scuttle my efforts? Didn't he know how much of myself I had invested? Didn't he care that both my wife and I had suffered with hepatitis in the pursuit of the research? Didn't he appreciate that some of Chile's leading student activists had supported our work?"

He obviously didn't know or care about these things. He only knew that he and many of his peers could have been in danger and that my government had a real interest in the issues I was pursuing. Later events were to show that he was right and that I, and not he, was the naïve and simple one.

## THE AMERICAN JURY SYSTEM

WHEREIN A GROUP OF LAWYERS AND SOCIAL SCIENTISTS
FROM THE UNIVERSITY OF CHICAGO RECEIVES PERMISSION
TO "BUG" ACTUAL JURY MEETINGS, RUNS AFOUL
OF A TIME-HONORED AMERICAN LEGAL TRADITION,
AND PRECIPITATES FEDERAL REGULATORY LEGISLATION.

The desire to collect potentially sensitive material often places the investigator in a vulnerable position as I had learned when conducting survey research in Chile. Intense suspicion and charges of betrayal by wary respondents have to be overcome. In the United States it is deemed inappropriate to record and analyze certain kinds of behavior without the explicit permission of those involved. When this occurs, the social scientist may face condemnation by officials who demand that he publicly reevaluate his own value assumptions. A fascinating case developed in the 1950s that pitted the value of freedom of research espoused by social scientists against that of the privileged communication among jurors as interpreted by two United States senators. The dramatic confrontation raised important questions of social science ethics that continue to be of importance and that have remained largely unresolved.

In 1952, members of the University of Chicago Law School embarked on a study of law and the behavioral sciences.[18] The research covered a wide variety of areas including the process by which juries reach their verdicts. The design of the investigation called for intensive interviews with jurors just *after* they had deliberated on a case and the use of mock trials in which the behavior of jurors could be closely observed. The proposal was then widely circulated to various members of the legal profession for comment. Paul Kitch, a lawyer in Wichita, Kansas, answered with a strongly worded critique that condemned the methodology as inadequate. Jurors, he argued, too often were inaccurate in their efforts to recall the process of their deliberations and the evidence that proved most conclusive. He cited previous studies to support his point that jurors were often unaware of their psychological motivation and, indeed, made distorted statements in order to please the interviewer. Kitch asserted that if the investigators really desired to break new ground, they would have to record *actual* jury deliberations and do a content analysis of these discussions. It would be possible, he thought, to secure permission for this from judges in Kansas.

In subsequent personal conversations with the Dean of the Chicago Law School and others, he offered to make the necessary inquiries. Dean Edward H. Levi and his staff agreed to follow Kitch's suggestion if he could secure permission. Kitch first approached Delmas C. Hill, Judge, U.S. District Court, and Orie L. Phillips, Chief Judge, U.S. Court of Appeals, Tenth Judicial District. He outlined an explicit and strict set of regulations governing the recording and safeguarding of selected jury deliberations. Central to the agreement was that control over the material would be exercised by the trial judge or his clerk. The recordings would be kept under lock and key in the judge's chambers and would not be released to the researchers until after the jury had completed its task and all subsequent appeals had been exhausted. Thus, the recordings in no way could affect the outcome of the case. Only then would the recordings be edited by one of the researchers. He would make certain to delete all material that could identify the proceedings in any way. This version would then be evaluated by the judge's representative who would have complete freedom to omit any other statements. The edited manuscript would be returned to the researchers while all other recordings or manuscripts would be destroyed. This careful procedure was designed to prevent any individual's identity from becoming public. Judge Phillips was still reluctant, and he suggested that the jurors' permission be secured. After further conversations he agreed to proceed without such permission and beginning in February 1954, six cases were recorded.

Soon afterwards, one of the social scientists associated with the project presented a paper based on one of the edited recordings to the annual conference of the Tenth Judicial Circuit. This act and the discussion that followed brought the secret recordings to public attention. The Internal Security Subcommittee of the Senate Committee on the Judiciary called a public hearing to delve into the implications of recording jury deliberations. Senators Eastland and Jenner, among the most politically conservative men on the committee, were the only two members present. Their questioning focused very heavily on the subversive aspect of tampering with a central feature of American life. They continually pressed academic witnesses with the gravity of the threat to the democratic system and rejected the argument that they had taken great precautions to preserve the integrity and anonymity within the jury process.

The leading researchers were bombarded with questions about their backgrounds, associations, and political beliefs. Senators Eastland and Jenner and Committee Counsel Swindbourne were determined to prove that the project was directed by men with a history of involvement with communist causes. The

Ford Foundation, which had handsomely supported the research, and the University of Chicago, which housed it, were also under suspicion.

The testimony provides a chilling reminder of the political climate that prevailed in the United States during the early 1950s. Against these charges implicit in the questioning, what defense did the researchers present? Dean Levi attempted to put forth the statements of numerous distinguished jurists that a study of the jury system could make a vital contribution to its reform. He insisted that all the researchers were aware and respectful of the sacrosanct nature of the jury in our juridical system and that the project was deeply committed to the importance of the jury and its central place in American society. Yet men and women involved in jury duty assume a vital *public* role. Their decisions have direct consequences for many others. How they go about reaching their conclusions and their responsiveness to a judge's direction are of deep public concern. Dean Levi described the reduced influence of juries in England and argued that knowledge of jury functioning could prevent a similar occurrence in this country. He explicitly rejected a debunking motive and asserted that the project had highly constructive goals in mind.

Paul Kitch testified about the initial reluctance of the project leaders. His influence had been crucial, he recalled, in convincing them that actual recordings were indispensable. The precautions that had been taken gave full protection to the jury members since their identities were guarded, Kitch maintained. The researchers were only interested in making general observations and obviously had no interest in exposing any individual juror's views.

Other witnesses agreed with Committee Counsel Swindbourne that large-scale "bugging" could, indeed, make juries reluctant to express their views fully. Yet, researchers argued, the recordings were to be limited, scrupulous care was to be taken with them, and the positive results of the project would far outweigh any possible detrimental impact.

The researchers' arguments were obviously not accepted by the investigating committee, their congressional colleagues, or President Eisenhower. A year later a bill was enacted into law making it a federal crime to record jury deliberations. The absolute sanctity of the jury room was deemed more important than the possible benefits to be derived from any social science research.

The heated controversy over the jury "bugging" involved a head-on confrontation between competitive value systems. Discounting that the Senate Internal Security Subcommittee seemed more intent in exposing "subversives" than in exploring a sensitive issue, a tension quite obviously often exists between the importance of acquiring knowledge and the rights of privacy. The use of hidden recorders certainly *could* have had a detrimental affect on future jury deliberations.

Are there pertinent ethical standards to which the researchers might have turned twenty years ago? Do they exist today? While clearly defined guidelines have not been drawn, an analysis of the research adventure does lead to certain helpful observations about deception and its relationship to ethical responsibility.

Acts of deception frequently occur in social science investigations. Social scientists are seldom entirely frank about the nature of their interests, often cloak their attitudes toward respondents, and almost always conceal the exact nature of their knowledge about the people they are studying. These masks seem an integral part of the researcher's role, but raise the serious ethical questions I posed earlier. Thus Whyte told most people in Cornerville that he was writing a history of the community.[19] He felt this was far simpler and more effective than outlining in detail the actual goals of the study. Pierre L. van den Berghe did not hesitate to tell the South African authorities that he was intent on documenting the remarkable economic progress of the nation. He said nothing of analyzing the apartheid system.[20] Berreman often feigned more knowledge than he actually had in order to induce respondents to confide in him.[21] Arlene Kaplan Daniels changed her natural demeanor so that her male informants would find her more attractive and less threatening.[22] Jerry Hyman consciously manipulated his respondents to gain access to the potlatch.

When those being studied are unaware of a hidden recording device, when any control over the situation is denied the respondent, the researcher passes into a new domain. At that point, he assumes an even heavier burden to defend the legitimacy of his activities against a variety of critics ranging from respondents, to colleagues, to public officials who can accuse him of illegitimately infringing on the rights of others.

In some cases researchers may argue that those being studied are performing a public function and cannot claim the normal rights of privacy. Thus Dean Levi and his associates could stress how important it is in a democracy to understand the actions of jurors and how valuable the data would be from actual recordings. The researchers may also assert that every precaution was taken to protect the unwitting respondents from exposure. Yet when in spite of these arguments the researcher continues to be heavily criticized, he cannot dismiss others as simply self-interested or unenlightened. He has taken a risk and may find himself labeled a dangerous deviant. His own deep doubts may have found expression in others. He must then pit his values and definition of appropriate behavior against those held by others. The roles are then reversed. The researcher, shorn of his own masks, is now under scrutiny. His task is to prove that his work merits support because it is of great potential value and that his discretion deserves confidence. This is often a formidable undertaking. No field worker should lightly assume the burdens inherent in the use of hidden recorders unless he is prepared to wage such a battle in defense of his work.

## IMPERSONAL SEX

WHEREIN HUMPHREYS DISGUISES HIMSELF TO
OBSERVE HOMOSEXUALS IN PUBLIC BATHROOMS AND IN THEIR HOMES,
COMES UNDER FIRE FROM JOURNALISTS AND SOCIAL SCIENTISTS ALIKE,
AND IS VIGOROUSLY DEFENDED BY COLLEAGUES ADVOCATING
COMPLETE FREEDOM OF RESEARCH.

To study important sectors of social life can necessitate decisions about the use of unorthodox research methods as the jury study reveals. While some social scientists have employed hidden recording devices, others have disguised themselves in order to probe into sensitive areas.[23] This technique also raises fundamental questions of social science ethics and again poses the issue of competing value systems.

Laud Humphreys' research is a prime example of the use of disguised observation and led to a heated debate on the appropriateness of such methods.[24] In pursuing his doctoral work at Washington University at St. Louis he studied the nature of homosexual relations between men who had been total strangers prior to their brief intimate encounter. Humphreys observed such meetings in park bathrooms ("tearooms"). Since a lookout is extremely useful to watch for police or other unfriendly strangers, the researcher was able to assume a role that provided both an identity and a key observation post. From his guard position, Humphreys watched hundreds of acts of fellatio and made careful, systematic records of some fifty interactions. With the assistance of an actual participant, he also gathered another thirty accounts. These gave him sufficient data to analyze the nature of the contact that occurred in the bathroom stalls.

For a more complete analysis, however, Humphreys wanted to collect information on the socioeconomic characteristics, family relationships, and psychological motivations of the participants. The attempt to collect these data created a new set of obstacles. Humphreys' resolution posed another array of ethical issues. Since most of the men entered and left the "tearoom" quickly, there was little opportunity for casual conversation that might be transformed into an interview. Humphreys pursued a complicated, disguised, and effective procedure in order to question them later. He traced automobile license numbers to locate the men's home addresses; allowed a year to lapse, changed his hair style, manner of dress, and car to avoid recognition; and only then introduced himself as a researcher involved in a study of community health patterns. Humphreys successfully interviewed these men in their own homes without, according to him, their ever being aware that he knew of their "tearoom" visits. To the best of Humphreys' knowledge, his presence seemed to pose no threat to them or their families, which was of crucial importance to the researcher.

Humphreys also gathered many valuable insights from those men whom he calls his "intensive dozen":

Four of them were persons who opened up in the course of the formal interviews and began talking about their homosexuality. This enabled me to apprise them of my real purpose. The other eight reached the level of co-operation much earlier. I was introduced to one by another graduate student. The others were persons, generally affable and of higher educational attainment, with whom I was able to strike up conversations on park benches and by automobiles just outside the tearooms. At first, these latter were "cruising me," but I maintained and developed the relationship in my desired direction by "putting them down" gently with the sort of excuses girls used to use with me, then following with an invitation to join me for a drink or coffee at some nearby facility with a less sexually-charged atmosphere. Once I felt we were to the "first name" stage and communicating, I let them in on my research pur-poses. The encouraging thing was that not one of these persons retreated at that point.[25]

Humphreys' data enabled him to describe the sociological attractions of this type of homosexual outlet: its anonymity precludes any commitment to the partner; many of the partici-pants can make a quick stop as part of their regular work day; normal family life can be maintained. On the basis of inter-view material, Humphreys also analyzed the various types of men who find satisfaction through "impersonal sex."

As a result of his research, Humphreys also painted a sym-pathetic portrait of the men. He argued vehemently that they present no danger to anyone. The harassment they often suffer stems from repressive and exploitative agents of social control:

I don't know what I would have done had my data revealed that tearoom encounters constitute a danger to society or that my respondents are sick, sick people. By the end of my first year of field work, I realized that such stereotypes are false. I suppose this is where my metaphysical assump-tions—or those of the underdog school—enter the picture. I believe it can safely be taken for granted that *anybody* (or any sort of behavior) that our society stigmatizes has to be pretty decent once you look below the surface. I think that human beings are basically good but stuck with a lousy bunch of cultural norms. The only people I don't care for are like clergy and senators, cops and judges, who think they have a commission to keep people conforming to those norms. Thus far, I have avoided studying the moral elite of our society; because I know I'd end up with such nasty conclusions from my data. I don't want to be forced into writing bad things about my respondents, so I study those who, on the surface, are most condemned.[26]

Soon after the completion of his dissertation, officials at Washington University at St. Louis began to raise serious questions about the methodology. Charges were levied that the disguised observations violated the stipulations of Humphreys' grant from the National Institute of Mental Health regarding the protection of subjects. The Chancellor of the university informed the NIMH of these concerns and asked that another grant largely earmarked for Lee Rainwater, Humphreys' dissertation adviser, be held up pending an investigation. Although this grant was later awarded and the university investigation of Humphreys dropped, these events were exacerbated by departmental tensions that, according to Humphreys, allowed the university administration to "clip the wings" of the sociology faculty.

The conflict between the sociology department and the university administration was publicized by a local newspaper. Humphreys relates the reactions of some of the men whose active help he had secured in his study:

By the next day, several of my cooperating respondents had phoned to ask if they were in any jeopardy. I assured them that no one was in danger of exposure, that all data containing any possibility of identification had been burned. When the furor arose, I had carefully destroyed all tapes and portions of the interview schedules that contained occupational and other traceable information. At first, I hid the master list in a safe-deposit box nearly a thousand miles distant. Eventually, after committing that to memory, it was also destroyed. They seemed fully satisfied with my assurances, and I asked them to pass the word around the local tearooms. I then set about to contact each of the remaining cooperating respondents. Subsequent contacts with these men, as well as with several others who later came to realize their role as subjects in my research, have left me confident that they remained unscathed by the negative publicity my work received.[27]

Yet it is crucial to emphasize that Humphreys' respondents knew full well that he had no legal means by which to keep the potentially explosive data from falling into the hands of police or other authorities. Humphreys' informants were totally dependent on his shrewdness. Social scientists, I would stress, are vulnerable to subpoena and, unlike physicians, lawyers, and clergy, cannot promise their respondents any legal immunity.

The subsequent publication of Humphreys' work in *Transaction* created another storm of controversy and became a topic of heated debate among social scientists, journalists, and other interested readers of the popular and prestigious social science journal. Nicholas von Hoffman, writing in *The Washington Post* (reprinted in *Transaction*), accused Humphreys of the same kind of blatant invasion of privacy as police are often charged with.[28] There are certain areas of personal life, according to von Hoffman, that are simply not the domain of the "snooping" social scientists. Von Hoffman discounted the precautions that Humphreys had taken to protect the identity of the men and asserted that Humphreys' material could have been used for blackmail.

Irving Louis Horowitz and Lee Rainwater, two social scientists most directly responsible for *Transaction*, and closely associated with Humphreys' work at Washington University at St. Louis, wrote a stinging retort to von Hoffman and all critics of unrestrained social science inquiry.[29] They maintained that the crucial issue centers on the right of the researcher to cast light into social areas hitherto covered by ignorance and darkness. The history of scientific research, they argued, is replete with instances in which investigators have been condemned for delving into what some considered private and sensitive areas. They commended Humphreys' scrupulous care in protecting the identity of those he studied and reiterated that, unlike policemen or journalists, social scientists are rarely interested in exposing particular individuals to public scorn or legal prosecution. On the contrary, the desire to generalize is the primary rationale for scientific research. Horowitz and Rainwater praised Humphreys for his courage in undertaking such pioneering research and argued that his findings could contribute to enlightened social policy.

There has been a great deal of controversy among social scientists about the appropriateness of Humphreys' research. Many lend support to the arguments put forth by Horowitz and Rainwater. A few have denigrated Humphreys as a mere pornographer because he described homosexual activities in clear detail. Certain associations are too private or unpleasant to publicize, the detractors seem to maintain. Personal revulsion, however, is not of primary concern. More pertinent questions concern the scientific relevance and ethical implications of Humphreys' study.

Did he select an important problem area? Humphreys reports that a high percentage of police arrests occur among those frequenting public men's rooms and yet nothing is known about these men, their background, work, and family life. Were Humphreys' methods directed toward careful collection of reliable data? His essay reveals a meticulous and sophisticated respect for social science research procedure. Did his work illegitimately infringe on the rights of those observed? Here, as I see it, the answer is far more complex and must be divided into the two major phases of the approach Humphreys followed. His first encounter with the men occurred in a *public* bathroom. He had as much right to be there as any of the participants. Indeed, as the lookout, he took the same risks as those he observed. Arrest, harassment, and physical violence could have been his lot.[30]

The situation was markedly different, however, in the second stage of the research design. Here Humphreys visited the men in their own homes. He watched them prepare barbecues, have their evening drinks, and converse with their families. Humphreys was an invited outsider. He took no personal risk by being there, but his presence did pose a potential threat to the men and their families. Humphreys' account is the only one available, and we do not know whether any of the respondents were frightened by the researcher's home visit. There has been no follow-up inquiry to alert us to any anxiety that they may have suffered as a result of the coverage that the research has received in the mass media.

Humphreys' decision to pursue the participants to their homes was a momentous one. He obviously believed that the blatant deception that he practiced was justified by scientific and policy returns. While it is difficult to evaluate this claim, it is apparent that social scientists assume a great responsibility when they deny respondents the rights of voluntary participation. What motivated Humphreys to utilize a method that he knew would raise the gravest ethical questions? The search for the answer provides important insight into the nature of the research craft.

Humphreys' own views on this issue merit full presentation and careful consideration. It is important to emphasize that Humphreys saw his own work as part of a long-standing tradition in American sociology. He clearly identified his professional reference groups, which, he felt, gave full legitimacy to his investigation. Like the social scientists who "bugged" the jury room, Humphreys' decision was very much influenced by many members of the profession. Humphreys was deeply enthusiastic about his graduate school experiences and their influence on him:

The years from 1965 to 1968 were wonderful ones at Washington University. Not only did we have a faculty that ranged from Al Gouldner and Jules Henry on the left to Bob Hamlin on the right, but a number of the great minds of the discipline were in the middle. The first two years I was there we had an unbelievable colloquium series. Each speaker would stay for two days of formal and informal discussion with the students. The first year we had Howie Becker, Erving Goffman, Talcott Parsons, Kai Erikson, Marty Lipset, Robin Williams, Everett Hughes. Next year, as I recall, we had Richard Flacks, Herbert Marcuse, Oscar Lewis, Gideon Sjoberg, B. F. Skinner, Al Cohen, and Ed Friedenberg. The atmosphere was one of constant intellectual challenge and stimulation, very rough and tumble. Everything developed in conflict. One *had* to defend his own views, long before he knew what they really were. We were expected to be original, imaginative, and controversial.

Now, in such an environment, there are no taboo topics or forbidden strategies. The only things condemned were irrelevance and dishonesty. Rainwater and Horowitz were my mentors. Lee Rainwater played a major role as my research director. It was he who suggested, kept pushing, and supported me in three major strategies: the use of systematic observation forms ("simple observation is not adequate; it must be disciplined and systematic"), sampling by means of recording license numbers, and structural interviews of the participant sample.

My sociological reference group was clearly of the naturalist-ethnographic-underdog school. Because of my background in the ministry, Becker was more of a hero than Goffman. I saw myself as an inheritor of a tradition from Mead and Simmel, the Chicago School, Dollard, the Lynds, William F. Whyte, Becker, Polsky, Goffman—but also of an anthropological tradition of Malinowski, Firth, Oscar Lewis, Jules Henry, and Elliot Liebow. Along with this tradition, I also saw myself as part of another—not quite so cool and somewhat more committed: Marx, C. Wright Mills, Paul Goodman, Friedenberg, Harrington, Horowitz, Christian Bay.

There is no question but that I see myself connected with (and sometimes pulled apart by) two very vital and legitimate sociological traditions. On the other hand, I do not make a good "party man." I can't think of a time I have ever been in the mainstream of anything. The cutting edge, yes—mainstream, no. For as long as I can remember, I have been a boundary tester. There was plenty of precedent for my research strategies; but Rainwater, Horowitz, Pittman—all of my advisers—and I agonized over every move, every step of the research. Nick Demerath and Helen Gouldner, among others, had serious doubts about my publishing the results. So, to be honest, I knew damned well that I was going out on a limb. But I also knew there would be those holding a net below when the limb was sawed off.[31]

Humphreys' prediction was not entirely without merit. His former professors and many of his colleagues ardently supported him when he was criticized for the subject and methods of his research. He was also honored by the Society for the Study of Social Problems when his book received the C. Wright Mills award as a major contribution to the study of critical social issues.

Yet other social scientists are far less sanguine about Humphreys' methods. Daniels, whose research on the military was discussed earlier, is particularly worried about the lack of ethical standards governing professional behavior and the resultant danger that faces unwary respondents or consumers. Her subsequent study of psychiatrists did not leave her any more reassured:

I have very grave doubts about the argument that we should rely upon Humphreys' personal sense of honor, ethics, or professional discretion, no matter how well developed these traits are in him. The point of a professional control structure is to obviate the necessity for depending upon individual integrity so entirely. In my opinion, no one in the society deserves to be trusted with hot, incriminating data. Let me repeat, *no one.* And that is because we should not have to rely upon the individual strength of conscience which may be required. Psychiatrists, for example, are notorious gossipers about the more "squidgy" aspects of patient life. They feel free to talk over details with associates because of their collegial relationship and mutual understanding of the rules of confidentiality.

O.K. So they mainly just tell one another. But they *sometimes* tell wives, people at parties, you and me. And few of them would hold up under systematic pressure from government or whatever to get them to tell. I understand there are many victims of the McCarthy era who are now heartily sorry that they told their psychiatrists about radical political interests. The issue is not that a few brave souls *do* resist. The issue is rather what to do about the few who will not? I think it is better to tell no one. And better to entrust no one (outside of the priesthood and people trained all their lives to hold up under secrets) with any "hot" material. There is *nothing* in our training—any more than in the training of psychiatrists, no matter what they say—to prepare us to take up these burdens.[32]

I need not completely subscribe to Daniels' harsh critique of contemporary professional ethics in order to point to the dangers inherent in Humphreys' research procedures. By his own account, he was willing to take risks and suffer the consequences for probing into the most private areas of human relationships through the use of most controversial methods.

My conversations with Humphreys convinced me of his extra-ordinary courage and ability to withstand condemnation and abuse. Yet these very characteristics make him a poor model for others to emulate without the most painful self-scrutiny. There are few social scientists who have such personality strength and commitment to the underdog. There are even fewer who combine these characteristics with Humphreys' research expertise. There are almost none who are also so completely assured of the ultimate importance of their efforts.

While admiring Humphreys, I know that I could not pursue such research myself and would attempt to dissuade others from such a path. The dangers to respondents, to the researcher, and to the precious sense of respect for the privacy of others seem too great for the returns. Had Humphreys faltered, had his data been secured by police officials or unscrupulous black-mailers, Humphreys would have been branded a rogue and a fool. He can now legitimately reject these epithets. Others, particularly those whom we hope to help by our efforts, should not be put in such jeopardy except with their explicit consent.

## Summary Discussion

The social scientist's primary goal is to unravel complex social relationships. This always entails probing beyond surface manifestations, raising sensitive questions, and overcoming respondent resistance. Whyte carefully nurtured informants throughout Cornerville in order to gather his data. He began his work by focusing on the structure of local gangs. His efforts later turned to more sensitive community-wide issues. Whyte made an important contribution to the sociology of corruption, and the relationship of the rackets to legitimate institutions remains an intriguing and explosive issue in contemporary American life.

Sexual mores also came under analysis. "A Slum Sex Code" provides ample insight into the varieties of definitions held by the street-corner men. Whyte again dealt with an area of vital interest to scientists and activists. The Women's Liberation Movement would find his work evidence for their battle cry against male sexual exploitation.

Although a white researcher, Liebow secured the confidence

of Tally and the other black men early in his stay. While never a total participant, he was successful in gaining significant insights into the men's world. Liebow's research focused on a currently crucial American controversy. What is the relationship between people and their poverty? Who is to blame for their condition? How do the poor adapt to it? The debate over these issues is pertinent to government policy makers, social reformers, militant revolutionaries, and, of course, to the poor themselves. Liebow places responsibility squarely in the laps of those whose decisions deprive black men of a living wage.

Berreman confronted the barriers raised by a caste system. To maintain the façade of ideal role relations demanded that the higher castes protect their public image. They attempted to prevent outsiders from gaining incriminating information. Berreman and his assistants breached the walls by interviewing low-caste members. Inadvertent admissions by high-caste people also proved enlightening. The researcher had to probe very gently to learn of illicit sexual practices, neglected customs, and illegal transactions. The entire caste system and the rationales that supported it were questioned by the investigator who successfully overcame continuous respondent resistance.

Jerry Hyman was determined to study the potlatch. He used his friendship with a local family and his knowledge of community norms to overcome strong opposition to his presence. Later, Hyman raised a series of devastating questions about his own conduct and about the very nature of field work relationships. Hyman pleaded guilty to manipulation and blatant deception and challenged his fellow field workers to examine their own procedures and motives.

Penina and I discovered potent opposition to our goal of probing the thoughts and activities of Chilean students. Some political leaders condemned our efforts as spying for a foreign power and vehemently rejected our claims to legitimacy. Knowledge in the hands of North Americans, a few charged, could only bring harm to Chile's progressive forces. Support from other activists salvaged our work. In the process we learned much about student views and national political tensions. Student concerns with future careers were vividly displayed. The anxiety about American intervention was graphically detailed, and we found that in moments of crisis "strangers" became lightning rods for ever-present hostility. Only the most consistent support from informants can protect the vulnerable "outsider" who must honestly scrutinize his own defensiveness.

Humphreys overcame the likely resistance of many respondents by simply not informing most of them of his research. Now that his work is published some will surely come to know of their involuntary participation in his study. Since they are dispersed and powerless, their reactions will have little impact on Humphreys or social science. Colleagues within his own field, however, have been more articulate and influential in debating the legitimacy of disguised observations.

Whyte, Liebow, Berreman, Hyman, Humphreys, my wife and I survived the field work. The social scientists studying the jury system fared less well. They engaged in a most challenging venture in attempting to record actual deliberations. Publicity of their activities resulted in their own trial by Senate investigators who charged that the sanctity of a fundamental American institution had been undermined. The researchers were vulnerable to the suspicions and critique of the Senate watchdogs.

Many crucial questions thus face social scientists as they study the lives of others. To what extent are researchers ethically bound to inform respondents about the nature of their interests? Are certain areas taboo? Are disguised observations permissible?

There is little doubt that the research process almost always involves some form of deception.[33] Few social scientists will tell informants the exact nature of their interests. To do this, researchers argue, would signal the type of answers desired.[34] The social scientist tries to minimize the amount of distortion that his presence and very questions induce. Beyond this, he continually attempts to prevent those he is studying from masking pertinent areas. In this sense all researchers can be at odds with all respondents. The intensity and boundaries of this struggle are, however, important to delineate.

Whyte and Liebow observed the most sensitive areas of community life. They asked questions often relegated to the physician, priest, or attorney. Yet, since others almost always knew them as researchers and had come to accept them as concerned human beings, the element of choice usually existed. Most respondents and informants trusted them. Even under these circumstances field workers should feel uneasy. Herbert

J. Gans has expressed his sense of guilt about taking mental notes in situations where others seemed to forget momentarily that he was a researcher.[35] Gans reminds us that there is no escape from the dilemmas in field research.

The perceptive field worker is always faced with certain ethical problems. For some researchers these questions are particularly grave. Have they been justified in consciously accumulating material through the total ignorance of those who provide it? At what point has an inappropriate infringement of privacy occurred? Humphreys and his defenders argue that no area should be neglected by social scientists just because of its sensitivity. Others who hold the same views have undertaken pioneering research in human sexuality but have gained the permission of the subjects. The issue is not only the sensitivity of the subject matter but also the nature of the methods used to examine it.

Uniform standards do not and probably cannot exist. Every profession relies on the internalization of ethical precepts by its members, the sanctioning power of professional organizations and public officials, and, of course, the weight of public opinion, which may directly affect the offending practitioner. There are grave questions as to the general effectiveness of these safeguards on professional conduct. Their efficacy in the shadowy areas of social science ethics may be even more uncertain.[36]

Many of those engaged in social science field work continue to tread a thin line. Their critics outside of social science often accuse them of disrespect for basic human rights. Their colleagues, at times, raise questions about the actual or potential harm they may cause others. These colleagues maintain that trust and respect are the crucial components in a research relationship. The researcher, they argue, must convince others not only that he is worthy of their support and that he can appreciate their reluctance to assist him, but also that he is at least competent to protect them from ridicule. Respondents, these colleagues continue, should be warned of any possible danger and should be the ones to make the choice about participation. When they refuse, as they sometimes will, the social scientist should, and usually can, find alternate respondents.

Social scientists who employ disguised methods of data collection insist, on the other hand, that these are perfectly permissible as long as they are utilized by competent and committed researchers. Bias, they argue, can often best be reduced when others are unaware that they are being observed. The social scientist must, of course, employ proper safeguards to protect the identity of unwitting respondents, but he would be derelict in his search for knowledge were he to neglect crucial areas of social life because of the resistance of respondents or the condemnation of colleagues or interested others.

The arguments will continue. Individual cases will, no doubt, be settled on their own merits. Often the relative power of involved groups will be the deciding factor as in the jury hearings. Social scientists are reluctant to set closely delineated lines to regulate their own behavior. They desire the flexibility to choose their own methods according to the nature of the research and their personal proclivities. This makes open and probing debate all the more essential. Social scientists are, justifiably, reluctant to spare others from intensive analysis. They must expose their own procedures to the same rigorous scrutiny. Honest reporting of methods and continuous debate among colleagues and students are essential for those engaged in the research adventure. Social scientists who use disguised techniques must stand ready to defend themselves before a wide array of critical audiences.

An ominous new ingredient has now entered the controversy. The recent disclosures of widespread military surveillance of civilians, the ever-growing use of phone tapping, and the burgeoning data banks on millions of American citizens gravely undermine the rights of free expression and privacy. For their own interest, social scientists should be among the staunchest defenders of these rights against the would-be censors and controllers. Social scientists should be scrupulously careful about contributing to the fast-growing reservoir of suspicion and distrust that plagues the United States in the closing decades of the twentieth century.

## NOTES

1. Erving Goffman, *The Presentation of Self in Everyday Life* (Garden City, N.Y.: Anchor Books, 1959).

2. Peter L. Berger, *Invitation to Sociology: A Humanistic Perspective* (Garden City, N.Y.: Anchor Books, 1963).

3. For an intriguing account of this probing process and its consequences, see Renée C. Fox, "An American Sociologist in the Land of Belgian Medical Research," in Phillip E. Hammond (ed.), *Sociologists at Work* (Garden City, N.Y.: Anchor Books, 1968), pp. 399–452.

4. William Foote Whyte, Appendix: "On the Evolution of Street Corner Society," *Street Corner Society* (Chicago: University of Chicago Press, 1955), pp. 320–325, paperback ed.

5. For an enlightening discussion of the relationship between crime and social mobility, see Daniel Bell, "Crime as an American Way of Life," in his *The End of Ideology* (New York: Free Press, 1960). Robert Merton's classic discussion of the political machine includes some penetrating observations on its relationship to the organized rackets. Robert K. Merton, "Manifest and Latent Functions," in his *Social Theory and Social Structure* (New York: Free Press, 1957).

6. Much of the current research on Latin American slum areas is reminiscent of Whyte's account and reflects his concerns and efforts. At a conference of the Latin American Studies Association, for example, one of the speakers reported his experiences in Venezuela. He and his colleagues were concerned with the structure of legal institutions in the Caracas slums. A distinguished Venezuelan jurist, whose advice was sought, attempted to dissuade the North Americans from even entering these areas. He was convinced that their very lives were in danger. The slums, he insisted, were inhabited only by cutthroats and prostitutes. The North Americans persisted, won acceptance, and quickly found an existent and effective body of legal codes that governed disputes in the community. A popular and distorted image of slum life had been dispelled.

7. Elliot Liebow, *Tally's Corner* (Boston: Little, Brown, 1967), p. 250.

8. *Ibid.*, p. 226.

9. Gerald D. Berreman, *Hindus of the Himalayas* (Berkeley: University of California Press, 1963), p. 252.

10. This event is evidently not a completely isolated occurrence as T. N. Madan observes:

To begin with, everybody was pleasant to me in the village of Utrassu-Umanagri in South Kashmir where I spent a year in 1957–58. Within a few weeks, however, I was able to anticipate who would be the most useful informants because of their knowledge, friendly disposition, communicative nature, and relative freedom from work. I tried to cultivate the friendship of these persons, only to discover later on that they had strained relations with some very influential members of the village community. The latter developed a deep suspicion that their own misdoings would find their way into my book and were not happy about my presence in the village, causing me quite some worry. At the same time they also tried to win me over to their side. ["Political Pressures and Ethical Contraints Upon Indian Sociologists" in Gideon Sjoberg (ed.), *Ethics, Politics and Social Research* (Cambridge, Mass.: Schenkman, 1967), p. 171].

11. Personal correspondence between Gerald D. Berreman and the author dated March 3, 1971.

12. Berreman, *Hindus of the Himalayas, op. cit.,* pp. 242–243.

13. This analysis is excerpted from an unpublished essay on the potlatch by Jerry Hyman, who is on the Smith College faculty.

14. *Ibid.*

15. Personal correspondence between Pierre L. van den Berghe and author dated July 26, 1971. For an important and thoughtful discussion on this and related issues see Herbert C. Kelman, *A Time to Speak: On Human Values and Social Research* (San Francisco: Jossey-Bass, 1968).

16. *Newsletter*, American Anthropological Association, II, 9 (November 1970).

17. Frank Bonilla and Myron Glazer, Appendix A: "A Note on Methodology. Field Work in a Hostile Environment: A Chapter in the Sociology of Social Research in Chile," *Student Politics in Chile* (New York: Basic Books, 1970), pp. 313–333.

18. *Recording of Jury Deliberations*, Hearings Before the Subcommittee to Investigate the Administration of the Internal Security Act and Other Internal Security Laws of the Committee on the Judiciary, United States Senate, Eighty-Fourth Congress, First Session, October 12 and 13, 1955 (Washington, D.C.: Government Printing Office, 1955). Also, Ted R. Vaughan, "Governmental Intervention in Social Research: Political and Ethical Dimensions in the Wichita Jury Recordings," in Sjoberg (ed.), *op. cit.,* pp. 50–77.

19. Whyte, *op. cit.,* p. 300.

20. Pierre L. van den Berghe, "Research in South Africa: The Story of My Experiences with Tyranny," in Sjoberg, (ed.), *op. cit.,* p. 185.

21. Gerald D. Berreman, *Behind Many Masks* (Ithaca, N.Y.: The Society for Applied Anthropology, 1962), pp. 18–19.

22. Arlene Kaplan Daniels, "The Low-Caste Stranger in Social Research," in Sjoberg (ed.), *op. cit.*, esp. pp. 274–276.

23. For a series of accounts employing a wide range of data collection devices, including some that raise fundamental ethical issues, see Jack D. Douglas (ed.), *Observations of Deviance* (New York: Random House, 1970).

24. Laud Humphreys, *Tearoom Trade* (Chicago: Aldine, 1970); and "Tearoom Trade: Impersonal Sex in Public Places," *Transaction* (January 1970), pp. 10–26.

25. Personal correspondence between Laud Humphreys and the author dated February 24, 1971.

26. *Ibid.*

27. *Ibid.*

28. Nicholas von Hoffman, Irving Louis Horowitz, and Lee Rainwater, "Sociological Snoopers and Journalistic Moralizers: An Exchange," *Transaction* (May 1970), pp. 4–8.

29. *Ibid.*

30. Other field workers have suffered serious personal violence while conducting their research:

> A Cornell graduate student said today she was clubbed by a policeman as she tried to film a police attack on demonstrators outside the Conrad Hilton Hotel here on August 28, 1968.
> Testifying at the Chicago conspiracy trial, Mrs. Sarah Diamant said she came here during the Democratic National Convention to take films for her doctoral dissertation comparing 19th-century abolitionists with current student activists.
> She said she, her husband and another Cornell student were filming and tape recording events in front of the Hilton Hotel when policemen charged into the demonstrators' rank, "beating people and pushing people up against buildings."
> "I saw one policeman rushing toward me," she said. "I motioned toward the microphone in my hand. I thought he would understand. But he hit me with his club around the neck and shoulders." [From *The New York Times*, December 11, 1969, p. 43. © 1969 by The New York Times Company. Reprinted by permission.]

31. Personal correspondence between Laud Humphreys and the author dated February 24, 1971.

32. Personal correspondence between Arlene Kaplan Daniels and the author dated July 30, 1971.

33. Melville Dalton, author of the well-known work *Men Who Manage*, describes in vivid detail his attempt to acquire salary scales and other confidential information from the firms on which he was doing research. He was successful in using secretaries to get him information to which he would not normally have been privy. Dalton openly acknowledges that an exchange of favors won their cooperation. For a fascinating and troubling account of his field work, see Melville Dalton, "Men Who Manage," in Phillip E. Hammond (ed.), *Sociologists at Work* (Garden City, N.Y.: Anchor Books, 1968), pp. 58–110.

34. A classic case involving the practice of deception in regard to research subjects occurred in a study of obedience. For a discussion of the research findings, see Stanley Milgram, "Behavioral Study of Obedience," *Journal of Abnormal and Social Psychology*, 67 (1963), 371–378. Ethical issues are also discussed in Leonard Bickman and Thomas Henchy (eds.), *Beyond the Laboratory: Field Research in Social Psychology* (New York: McGraw-Hill, 1972).

35. Herbert J. Gans, "The Participant-Observer as a Human Being: Observations on the Personal Aspects of Field Work," in Howard S. Becker, *et al.* (eds.), *Institutions and the Person* (Chicago: Aldine, 1968), pp. 300–317.

36. For a perceptive and critical discussion of the problems of disguised observation, see Kai T. Erikson, "A Comment on Disguised Observation in Sociology," *Social Problems*, 14 (Spring 1967), 366–373.

# CHAPTER IV

## (A)

# the dimensions of reciprocity

The investigator's work does not end after he has completed the collection of his data. The task of evaluating his material still lies before him, and this may often prove a difficult and lonely intellectual challenge. Our major concern here, however, is with the extent to which the researcher experiences a sense of indebtedness to sponsors, informants, and respondents. Will his interpretation of the material be unduly influenced by the sponsors' interests, the informants' needs, or the respondents' sensitivities? How can the social scientist prevent such considerations from biasing his report? What kinds of compromise have occurred because the investigator gave in to illegitimate demands for reciprocity?

An analysis of this stage of the field work process uncovers the final dimensions of reciprocity. These include clear-cut and legitimate demands for *personal* reciprocity by respondents who expect that the field worker will have kept faith with them by protecting their anonymity and by preventing their exposure to ridicule or retaliation. It is not unknown for respondents and informants to voice displeasure about the manner in which they have been presented in the field worker's report, and it is not uncommon to hear their cries of betrayal. The researcher may even need to defend his scholarly competence publicly.

Beyond questions of personal reciprocity lies the often compelling issue of reciprocity to the entire *group* under study. Social scientists are becoming ever more aware that their writings can particularly influence the nature of public opinion and public policy toward disadvantaged groups. Many researchers, as a result, are now heavily engaged in debating the exact nature of their obligation. Should research findings be published when they may be misinterpreted to reinforce the negative image already held of certain groups? Do field workers have the right to gamble with the fragile attempt being made to uplift the conditions of America's oppressed? Conversely, must the concerned researcher now direct his efforts to help the less influential by putting his services directly at their disposal? Should the investigator interpret reciprocity to *groups* as the call to reinterpret the value and consequences of scholarly detachment? Shouldn't social scientists aid those whose need is so great in the most direct manner possible?

The dimensions of reciprocity go beyond evaluating obligations to *persons* and *groups*. They also may include the demands of powerful respondents or sponsors who may invoke *bureaucratic* reciprocity. The field worker is not immune to the pressures that may be applied to him or his superiors by influential administrators. When they have served as respondents, these men may seek revisions in the investigator's report analyzing their organization. When they have sponsored research, they may subtly or overtly attempt to influence the direction of the researcher's efforts and the contents of the findings. In either case, many social scientists face potent challenges to their own sense of scholarly independence.

Obviously, not all of these dimensions of reciprocity are faced by every investigator. Their significance varies markedly with the type of research that he has conducted. But many of the questions raised above trouble the social scientist as he enters the last stages of his research effort. For some investigators, these questions remain haunting ones of conscience long after the other problems of field work have faded from memory.

## CORNERVILLE

WHEREIN WHYTE RETURNS TO THE ITALIAN COMMUNITY
TO GARNER REACTIONS TO HIS BOOK AND FINDS THAT
THE EXPOSURE OF SENSITIVE ISSUES CAN BE DIFFICULT
FOR BOTH THE OBSERVED AND THE OBSERVER.

After the completion of his report, the field worker may quickly learn that his research is not entirely without cost. Some respondents may be pained by their reflection on the printed page. They may question whether the investigator has not used them and their community. The sensitive and concerned field worker will attempt to answer their implied criticism. He will also seek solace and gratification in the positive reactions of other subjects and in his own belief in the honesty of his effort. From these encounters, with others and with himself, the field worker comes to know that not even the most skillful presentation of data releases him from responsibility to those whom he has studied. He will long ponder what contribution, if any, he has made to people whom he has come to know so well.

William Foote Whyte was very much concerned about the impact of his book on his Cornerville friends.[1] Doc, of course, as a major figure in the study, had been placed in an embarrassing position. It was well-known that he had given essential support to Whyte's efforts and had provided him with many key insights into the functioning of local community life. Finally, known only to Whyte, Doc had gone over every page of the manuscript. Doc knew that some of the statements would be difficult for others to read, and yet he felt that they were an integral part of the situation.

Whyte fully sympathized with Doc's concern that the low-status members of the group would be particularly hurt by the public exposure of their position. In order to minimize the consequences, Doc tried to discourage people from reading the book. He also convinced a local newspaperman that running a column on it would make unprofitable copy.

Reactions varied among those who did read the book.

One or two jokingly kidded Doc about his portrayal as a man with great leadership ability. A local social worker, however, condemned Whyte for turning his back on his friends and making many unkind observations about them. Chick Morelli felt that Whyte had not sufficiently emphasized that the Cornerville gang was very young, that their actions had simply been those of kids growing up. Perhaps of most importance, Morelli felt that Whyte had caught the Cornerville people with their defenses down. He had written too much about the kinds of things that they might have preferred to keep quiet.

Whyte responded quite differently to these varying reactions. He rejected the statement of the social worker that he had sold out his friends for personal gain. Indeed, he reaffirmed his previous conclusion that the local settlement house was ill-equipped to deal with the problems of the Cornerville men and that its staff had little basis upon which to criticize his efforts. Whyte now believes that his observations about the importance of indigenous leadership may have been the most immediately practical ones in the entire book:

It just seems that this idea came some twenty years too soon. It is now becoming more and more recognized that, in dealing with low-income people, the roles that link the people with a social agency should be played by local people who have social skills and intelligence but don't have the formal educational qualifications usually required.[2]

Chick's accusation that Whyte had occasionally presented community people in a critical light was better founded. Every investigator who spends long periods in the field will uncover and present information that some of his respondents will find difficult to accept. His task is to go beyond the favorable image that they may wish to present, and he must often make public what they may prefer to keep private. His primary loyalty is not to a handful of informants but to a wider audience. The charge that he has observed and written about sensitive issues is usually accurate.

The statement that he has been overly critical can only partially be tested in a direct confrontation between researcher and informant. It is unlikely that those who feel abused will find complete satisfaction. Telling it "like *you think* it is" may be excellent advice in the abstract; it is almost always painful to someone in the concrete situation.[3]

Even at the last stage of the research process, Whyte clearly experienced the pains and joys of his field work efforts. He hoped that those of his friends who read his book would feel that he had been fair to them, and he respected their expectations of *personal* reciprocity. Yet, he knew that he had pulled no punches in his analysis of the data. He hoped, moreover, that the book might help some of them in making their way, but he was aware how little effect he could have on their lives. Chick Morelli, Doc assured him, had now seen himself as others did. Few people had that opportunity and he was a better man for it. Sam Franco, who had been of great help to Whyte, decided to pursue a research career and, after much difficulty, found a place for himself within the military. Years later, I have been told, he warmly boasted to a visiting sociologist about his role in Whyte's work. Doc, who received Whyte so openly, was quite successful in later years. Whyte recalls:

. . . for a while Doc did get some satisfaction out of being asked to talk to classes at Wellesley, but he tired of this and let me know that he did not want me in the future to tell people who he was and where he could be reached. But he did go on to get a job at Raytheon, and, the last I heard from him, he was superintendent of production control, which is a pretty responsible management position. A student tells me Doc died a couple of years ago.[4]

But what of Cornerville itself? Did those who played smaller parts in the action so faithfully recorded benefit at all? What of the many nameless people who crossed Whyte's path but failed to make their way into his pages? Did his efforts fail them? Should they have received more from his stay there? No precise answer can be found in Whyte's account. Yet looking back at his research encounters after more than a quarter of a century, Whyte seems fairly sanguine:

At least, it seems to me, the researcher has the responsibility to avoid doing the community harm and avoid harming the lives of the individuals he studies. As far as I can tell, I did meet that responsibility. Beyond that, a study might contribute to a broader understanding not just of Cornerville but of areas like it.[5]

Generations of students are indebted to the young Harvard scholar for delineating the complex organization of social life. Someone who has read *Street Corner Society* can approach Cornerville or any community with a sense of appreciation for the variety of human efforts striving to come to terms with their surroundings.

Is that enough? Did Whyte, in his effort to gain acceptance and cooperation, promise more than he could ever fulfill? Shouldn't social scientists attempt to be more accurate in predicting the fruits of their labors? Isn't it appropriate for field workers to alert respondents that their cooperation is basically an act of friendship and faith? Shouldn't Whyte's impressive and important study serve as a constant reminder just how ineffective most research projects are in uplifting the people in the community under analysis? Isn't it abundantly clear that researchers are woefully limited in influence, energy, time, and, indeed, interest? Shouldn't social scientists face up to the realization that their own careers are seldom built on dedication to the well-being of obscure communities? Isn't it true that no matter how sincere, the successful investigator's investment can only be ephemeral? The answer to some of these painful questions can be found in the cases that follow.[6]

## SPRINGDALE

WHEREIN VIDICH AND BENSMAN ARE CRITICIZED
BY PROFESSIONAL COLLEAGUES AND TOWNSPEOPLE ALIKE
FOR INDISCRETION AND EVEN MALICE AND RESPOND
BY REASSERTING THEIR OWN SENSE OF SCHOLARLY ETHICS.

The astute field worker can always be accused by some subjects of being unnecessarily harsh in his observation of community life. A powerful rejoinder, as Whyte learned, derives from the support and acclaim of subjects and colleagues who applaud his insights and thoroughness. When most of his subjects stand solidly against him and many of his fellow field workers condemn him, the researcher is in a difficult position. He may back down and admit the error of his ways or, on the contrary, take the offensive and scold all those who seek to question the legitimacy of his efforts. The beleaguered researcher may proclaim that his detractors are defensive precisely because his insightful account spares no sensitive area. He may insist that social science demands a commitment to exactly such hard-nosed analyses. Finally, he may argue he is the champion of unfettered research while his critical colleagues are simply the captives of expediency. In this situation, the field worker clearly and forcefully rejects the significance of *personal* reciprocity and claims that such considerations are simple encumbrances.

There have been important instances when social scientists have been roundly condemned for the results of community studies and, particularly, for being impervious to what others consider the legitimate demands for *personal* and *group* reciprocity. A classic case involves *Small Town in Mass Society*, published in the late 1950s.[7] The writers, Arthur Vidich and Joseph Bensman, have been criticized by some of the townspeople for grave distortion in describing and analyzing their lives and for indiscretion in presenting the material. This confrontation is a prime example of the sharp disputes that have arisen about the nature of reciprocity in research relationships. It is of particular interest for this discussion, since one of the first salvos was fired by Whyte, at that time editor of the social science journal *Human Organization*.

Whyte was particularly concerned about two issues: the relative ease with which some of the major community figures could be identified despite the use of pseudonyms and the extent to which individual researchers had access to the data collected by a team project. A number of crucial background factors spurred Whyte's probing questions.

The study was conducted in a small community near Cornell University by a large group of social scientists affiliated with Cornell. The university as a whole was very much concerned with maintaining a cordial relationship with Springdale's citizens. Indeed, a number of Cornell administrators, faculty, and staff resided there and were particularly sensitive to an upsurge of hostility toward the academic community. In addition, the townspeople had been consistently assured of "anonymity" by the investigators. Although there had been no official project policy on this matter, cooperation had been secured and reinforced by the promise that the report would be largely presented in statistical terms, which would dilute the possibility of identifying particular individuals. Finally, the researchers had clearly stated that the project was primarily concerned with the "constructive" manner in which the community adapted to meet its problems. It was suggested that the findings might help other communities with their difficulties.

Vidich, who served the project as field director, and Bensman, who had no direct involvement with Cornell or the data collection, redefined the theoretical goals of the study after Vidich left Cornell. Their work focused on the extent to which Springdale had been deeply affected by changes in the rest of American society. Vidich and Bensman described Springdale's institutions as deeply dependent on external ones and its value system, prized by the community for its indigenous and pure quality, as a mere reflection of the predominant beliefs of the mass society. Moreover, the authors observed, there was little substance to the claim that democratic participation and values flourished in Springdale. On the contrary, the authors wrote, major decisions were made by a few powerful individuals who were characterized as the "invisible" power holders.

Vidich and Bensman's incisive account of the community social structure was condemned by some colleagues for its breach of "professional ethics" and excoriated by many townspeople who charged the authors with brutal and irresponsible use of gossip and unsubstantiated material. Vidich, it was agreed by both groups of critics, had been received warmly in the community as field director and participant observer and had repaid his hosts by exposing them to national ridicule.

These accusations are reminiscent of some of those cast at Whyte after the publication of his Cornerville study fifteen years earlier. Why did these charges receive such prominence in this instance? What factors differentiated Whyte's work from that published by Vidich and Bensman?

Whyte was a lone, independent researcher studying an obscure Italian community, few of whose residents read his work. Vidich participated in a university research unit investigating a nearby community whose leading citizens read the published account. The outrage of concerned respondents had to be heeded and examined.

Vidich, himself, later acknowledged that he had been party to deceptive assurances about the protection of identities. He wrote that he had always doubted that the report would finally be presented in statistical terms but did not contradict his colleagues when they made this claim in order to assuage growing respondent anxiety about the project. Vidich also had little patience with the argument that some individuals had been hurt by his analysis. For him, this was the price inherent in contributing to knowledge. Vidich and Bensman rejected the project director's suggestion that they omit certain material in their manuscript that some townspeople might find objectionable. This, the authors felt, was unwarranted and unacceptable censorship. Vidich charged that it was a public relations rather than a scholarly consideration. The very nature of the research, Vidich argued, risked exposing some people. While the standard precautions of pseudonyms had been taken, he had known they would be insufficient to hide the identity, for example, of a mayor or the town council. Their roles were too public and their positions too easy to recognize.

Vidich and Bensman argued that the scholar could not distort the accuracy of his data in an attempt to disguise the identities of public functionaries. Moreover, they legitimately argued that the report published by the project had used the same pseudonyms they had created. My own reading of the controversy leads me to conclude that the project leaders and townspeople were more angered by the critical portrait Vidich and Bensman painted of Springdale and actually less sensitive to the issue of identification of prominent townspeople than they claimed.

Vidich and Bensman were unyielding in their commitment to their own sense of scholarly integrity. They vehemently rejected those who, according to them, would dictate the tone or the direction of their analysis. They accepted the possibilities that an insightful document can injure the sensibilities of some of those under study. But they refused to be stampeded by the complaints of influential people who had the ear of university officials and faculty. I support their forthright stand on this issue.

On the other hand, the authors have never given sufficient justification to one crucial criticism of their work. The research relationship, as all others, includes a distinctive set of legitimate expectations. In seeking assistance, the researcher invariably bargains with those he wants to study. He promises certain considerations for the favors received. These may often include assurances of complete anonymity. Where this is unacceptable, because of the nature of the study, the researcher must make it quite clear.

From my perspective, none of the Springdale researchers, Vidich and Bensman included, is completely guiltless. Vidich implicitly agreed to certain limitations and then cried foul when townspeople demanded that he live up to them. The quest for understanding of other people's lives is not a license to reject *any* responsibility for their well-being.[8] A cavalier response to a weighty criticism does not settle the issue. It simply means that in this instance the power rests with the researcher. Others can do little to prevent his publishing his material. It is not always so.

## CHILE

WHEREIN I RETURN TO IDYLLIC PRINCETON TO COMPLETE
THE DIFFICULT ANALYSIS OF MY DATA AND LEARN, ALMOST
IN PASSING, THAT THE SUSPICIONS OF OUR CHILEAN CRITICS
WERE, INDEED, NOT TOTALLY WITHOUT FOUNDATION.

Field workers returning from overseas research often suffer a reverse form of culture shock. They find it difficult to readapt to the life style of their own country. They must occasionally confront the consequences of their own subordinated position. Graduate students particularly may learn how dependent they are on the decisions of senior professors who control fellowship funds. Thus, while some social scientists may minimize their indebtedness to subjects, others become deeply concerned by their seeming inability to repay hosts for their acceptance, support, and cooperation.

Since my research method emphasized the use of structured interviews and my findings were presented primarily in statistical terms, I had less worry about hurting particular individuals than did Whyte or the Springdale researchers. Despite the fears of some of my respondents, there was no possibility that any one person could be identified. My concerns about *personal* reciprocity were, nonetheless, quite pressing. How would key informants react to the report? Would they think that I had successfully captured the essence of Chilean student life? I was deeply concerned with keeping faith with my Chilean friends and had consistently affirmed my belief that the research could contribute to a better understanding of Chilean youth. Would those who had risked their reputations to help me find my work satisfying? They had their own views and strong commitments. Would they define my critical analysis of certain aspects of student political life as a betrayal of their confidence? Would they think I had seduced them into trusting me? Would they feel exploited by the return on their investment? Had I presented an overly sympathetic and nonjudgmental image to them as a result of my own need to maintain their support?

Since we remained in Chile two months after the collection of the data, I had some opportunity to discuss the initial findings with friends and informants. I also corresponded with them during the year it took to complete the writing of the study. After the dissertation was completed, I sent copies to Chile and discussed it in detail with several Chilean friends who had come to pursue graduate work in the United States. I also showed them drafts of articles that I was preparing to publish in Spanish- and English-language journals. The Chileans' critical comments were often incorporated into the work.

While there were differences of opinion on certain interpretations, there was general agreement on the major focus of the analysis. I had clearly detailed the concern that most of the students expressed with their professional training, the desire of the political activists to use their skills to uplift the life of the urban poor, their simultaneous resistance to working in the countryside, and the negative impact that student strikes had on the quality of university life. I had not spared enthusiasm for, or criticism of, the students' attempts to confront the difficult realities of Chilean national life in the mid-1960s. I had enough respect for all the Chileans we knew to tell the story as fairly as I could. There was no request among our Chilean supporters for any toning down or modification of the reports and apparently no desire for any such modification.

Unlike Whyte, I strongly hoped that many Chileans would read the work. I felt that this was the most legitimate form of reciprocity for all the help and encouragement that we had received. To facilitate this end, copies of the published articles were placed at several libraries at the University of Chile and distributed to the dozen or so people who had been most interested in the research.

I have, however, pondered and brooded about other questions, which have a direct bearing on the issue of *personal* as well as *group* reciprocity. While in Chile, we had often discussed the importance of our country's reaction to events in Latin America. Many Chileans had been deeply concerned about the direction of United States foreign policy, the threat of military intervention or economic sanctions in the event of a leftwing victory in the presidential election. Could my research, and the work of other investigators, reveal to our policy makers the depth of desperation that many Chileans felt about their country's situation? The need for broad social change was imperative if thousands of Chileans were to secure a share of their nation's wealth. Had I deluded myself about the possible impact of social science research? Was anybody in Washington listening? I received a surprising and rather unpleasant answer to that query, which again raised the sensitive issue of research sponsorship and its direct relationship to questions of reciprocity.

My grant from the private Doherty Foundation had terminated at the end of June, and, during my last two months in Santiago, I had been supported by the Center of International Studies at Princeton University. I had received permission to remain in Chile until the presidential election and had been assured time and use of center facilities to complete my report when I returned to the United States. This arrangement had seemed excellent, and I was pleased to be associated with the prestigious center. We left Santiago on September 4, 1964, the day the Christian Democratic candidate was elected President of Chile.

Princeton seemed so far from Santiago. No poster-lined walls, no slums, and no mass rallies were to be found there in 1964. The field work adventure was over, but the hard task of completing the study remained. Perhaps, I thought, it was better to be away from Santiago. Quiet and time for reflection were so important for a careful review of the data. It would be easier to write objectively. A sense of distance was crucial to maintain the proper perspective. I almost convinced myself that the feelings of depression would soon pass and that, in time, I would find myself reaccustomed to the sedentary life of the library scholar.

My growing sense of inner tranquillity abruptly ended, however, during my first conversation with the director of the center. He informed me that while I was, of course, completely free to pursue my writing, I did have one minor obligation. Since my work was now being supported by SORO (an Army sponsored research unit), I had to file a quarterly report on my progress.

I was stunned by this revelation. While in Latin America I had bristled at accusations that my wife and I had official government connections, and I had assured the Chileans that my funds had been provided by a private foundation. Now I learned that the coveted center grant, which had supported my last two months in Chile, had been provided, in actuality, by the United States Army.

I told the director about my experiences in Chile, my solemn declarations of nongovernment support, and my personal feeling that military funds were absolutely inappropriate to support overseas research. The center's arrangement with SORO was its own affair. While in Santiago, I had been offered a position on the center staff with the stipulation that my only obligation and consideration would be to write my doctoral dissertation. I stated, therefore, that I would submit progress reports to him, but that I refused to have any contact with SORO. My major concern was with keeping faith with the Chileans, which I could do only by scrupulously maintaining my independence.

The statement served to ease my conscience for the moment. My work was still free from military interference. Nobody would influence my analysis, and no sponsor could demand any changes in the findings or modifications in the interpretation. Yet the situation continued to disturb me. I felt duped by my ignorance and disgusted by what seemed to be the ubiquity of Department of Defense presence.

Immediately afterward, I spoke at length to a distinguished and knowledgeable professor working in the area of comparative studies. He advised against making an issue of the funds. What was the difference, he asked, between my situation and that of a well-known and sincere Princeton radical who gave lectures to cadets and faculty at the War College? It was essential to recognize how important the military were and try to influence them. You remained completely free, he continued, to say or write anything you pleased. The manner in which the center grant had been awarded to me had been an error in judgment. I should have been informed of the source of the funds. Nonetheless, he continued, the SORO grant had been allocated directly to the center. I had been awarded an assistantship by the center board and had *nothing* to do with any outside group.

I accepted this argument, but, although I completely dissociated myself from any non-university agency or influence, I have remained uneasy about the remarkable turn of events and my response to it. They are symptomatic of deep-seated and unresolved problems of social science ethics and expose how sensitive and subtle the question of reciprocity can be when powerful sponsors are involved. I am still haunted by the knowledge that several copies of my dissertation were forwarded by the center directly to SORO.

I continue to be deeply disturbed by the role played by the center and my distinguished consultant. By what rationale could the center have accepted a grant from a research agency of the United States Army and bestowed it upon a student doing field work in a Latin American country? The answer, I believe, lies in the extent to which major United States universities were willing to compromise themselves following World War II. Funds were crucial for the creation and survival of prestigious and expensive research institutes. The Department of Defense became a major benefactor. Far too many well-known and respected administrators and scholars saw no conflict between their avowed commitment to unfettered social science inquiry and to the liberation of exploited peoples, on the one hand, and their willingness, on the other, to serve the interests of the American military by accepting its research funds and making reports directly available to its analysts. Only later, when the Vietnam War had made any association with the military utterly unpalatable, did these academic men and women begin to reexamine their actions and assumptions. By then, however, it was too late to convince skeptics here and abroad that social scientists could really be trusted. For the right price, it seemed patently clear, many in the American university community had become subservient to the wielders of national wealth and power.[9]


## INDIA

WHEREIN BERREMAN PUBLICLY DENOUNCES PENTAGON
SPONSORSHIP OF A PROJECT WITH WHICH HE HAD BEEN ASSOCIATED
AND FINDS THAT HIS DISCLAIMER DOES NOT PUT HIM ABOVE
SUSPICION BY INDIAN OFFICIALS INCREASINGLY
WARY OF UNITED STATES ACADEMICS.


While some social scientists reluctantly, but ultimately, accept financial support from sources they consider inappropriate, others respond far more effectively. It is rare, but fortunately not unknown, for a field worker to resign from a project for reasons of conscience. His decision often rests on the significance of reciprocity and the importance of maintaining the distinction between social science and intelligence gathering. When he makes his views public, however, he runs the risk of offending colleagues who may charge him with attempting to scuttle their work. The researcher may also be required to defend his judgment to critical government officials in other countries.

After the completion of his book, Gerald D. Berreman sent copies to his two assistants. They, in turn, showed the photographs and summarized or translated sections to villagers from Sirkanda who visited them in town. Berreman also sent a copy of the book to the village teacher, mostly as a sentimental gesture, since the teacher could speak or read no English. According to Berreman, personal reciprocity, then, took more the form of being "straight-forward with the people and not betraying their trust":

I returned ten years later and was gratified, even overwhelmed, to find how positively they responded to me—how nostalgically they remembered my stay there a decade earlier. They were more hospitable upon my return than they ever had been during my residence in the village! I attribute this to the fact that none of their anxieties about my presence proved to have been warranted and moreover, of course, those were times when people now dead were alive and when there was a certain optimism about the future, now dissipated—so the times were remembered somewhat fondly.[10]

Despite his reception, Berreman, realistically and legitimately, is quite unsure if he ever had the ability to fulfill his promise to help the people of Sirkanda. In the preface to the second edition of his book, Berreman candidly admits how ineffectual his efforts have been:

My ultimate thanks go again to the people of Sirkanda. I have learned much from them and have benefited in many ways from our unlikely friendship. I wish I believed that the benefits were mutual. I do not, for while I provided them with some momentary diversion and perhaps some amusing or even valued memories, I could not help them directly with the chronic or acute problems of their lives. I can only hope that this book, by portraying them respectfully, sympathetically and realistically to others—as I have tried to do—will reach and influence those with power to affect their lives, and so repay in part the debt I owe them.[11]

Berreman also faced the issue of *bureaucratic* reciprocity in research relationships several years after his research in Sirkanda, when he, too, confronted the thorny issue of sponsorship. His experiences illustrate the significant impact that Department of Defense funds had on social science research during the 1960s and the traps to which field workers were exposed when they became associated in any way with this agency.[12]

According to a report in *The New York Times*, Indian officials in 1968 became deeply suspicious of all United States visitors to their nation when it was revealed how many American private foundations, labor organizations, and student groups had been receiving support from the Central Intelligence Agency. After learning about research sponsored by the Department of Defense in India from a letter that Berreman wrote to the Senate Foreign Relations Committee, one Indian leader "charged that the Pentagon and the C.I.A. were busy infiltrating spies into the Himalayas, not only as scholars, but also as artists, bird-watchers, and yogies."[13] As a result of these and other accusations, Berreman's own request for permission to return to India was challenged by wary officials. They particularly wanted information on his relationship to the American military and intelligence authorities. He was asked to explain his recent association with a Pentagon sponsored "research project on the Himalayas." Berreman had immediately dissociated himself from the project after learning about the nature of the funding, and he had sent "Senator J. W. Fulbright, Chairman of the Foreign Relations Committee, a copy of a letter he had written withdrawing from participation." That letter protested Department of Defense funding, cited the danger it posed to American research in South Asia, and predicted the repercussions likely to follow if the funding were sustained—repercussions that, in fact, occurred shortly thereafter. This public disclosure was in accordance with Berreman's sense of appropriate scholarly behavior, but it apparently did not completely satisfy the Indians. Further detailed explanation was necessary before Berreman could convince his hosts of his legitimate scholarly interests.

Thus, although Berreman had previously been in India and had written a respectable and scholarly account of village life, he was not immune to charges of spying. The lesson is clear. Hosts are now more adamant in their demand that reciprocity for their assistance include the greatest respect for their sovereignty. American researchers may continue to be welcome only if they more fully appreciate these legitimate sensitivities.[14]

Indeed, Berreman and other social scientists have made some harsher observations and far less palatable predictions. Scholars and political activists in other countries may soon demand far greater control over the accumulation and use of knowledge within their own borders. Charges of "research colonialism" or "academic imperialism" against Americans have already been heard.[15] United States social scientists are being charged with monopolizing data collection because of their superior numbers and abundance of financial support.[16] Foreign critics accurately state that the advantages of social science research most often accrue to powerful nations. Berreman believes that in Asia, Western scholars may have to learn to play a subordinate role as local researchers, more oriented to national considerations, specify what aspects of social life are to be studied and what is to be done with the findings.[17] While this may be a bitter pill for those committed to the current definition of professional control, it may soon be the only realistic alternative to total exclusion from certain countries.

Berreman has also raised other disturbing questions about the anthropological enterprise overseas.[18] He has criticized some of his colleagues for pursuing secret counterinsurgency-oriented research in Thailand during the late 1960s and has sided with the younger and more radical anthropologists in their goal of making their profession far more cognizant of its role in furthering American foreign policy. Berreman and other critics have strongly advocated the importance of greater sensitivity on the part of anthropologists to the use of their findings. Expressions of scholarly "neutrality," the critics charge, simply camouflage the reality of contemporary world power relations. Anthropologists and other social scientists, according to Berreman, must honestly ask themselves why they are doing certain kinds of research, who will benefit from the findings, and what impact the investigation will have on those studied. More to the point, Berreman argues, anthropologists must dedicate themselves to serving their own version of a better world. The profession, he feels, is now controlled by those who are willing to serve American national power and who are reluctant to answer the potent thrusts of the radical members.

Other anthropologists like Delmos J. Jones, who did field work in Thailand, have faced the prospect that their research on the hill people may very well have been used by the Thai government for manipulative and coercive ends.[19] Jones charges that it is the responsibility of anthropologists *not* to publish when their findings can be used against those studied. To be sure, he writes, refusal to publish may be professionally self-destructive for any given anthropologist. Career rewards are intimately tied to production. Yet Jones asserts that sincerely concerned scholars must pay the price for their beliefs. My own experiences in Chile and elsewhere in Latin America lead me to support and embrace this position.

## VIETNAM

WHEREIN RAMBO LEADS A TEAM OF RESEARCHERS
ON A MILITARY SPONSORED PROJECT, INADVERTENTLY LEARNS
ABOUT TERROR PRACTICED AGAINST CIVILIANS, AND RELATES
THE RESPONSE OF UNITED STATES AUTHORITIES TO HIS PROTEST.

Although many social scientists shrink from accepting military funds to support their research, there are others who actively identify with their nation's military policies. Some have become participants in the Vietnam War. They have believed that their skills could help defeat a ruthless enemy with the capability to impose a totalitarian form of life on a reluctant people. The conflict over reciprocity has involved some of these committed researchers in the most agonizing of decisions. They have been forced to reevaluate their position as the human costs of the war have skyrocketed beyond the imaginations of all but the most involved.

The competing demands of reciprocity are nowhere more tragically revealed than in the work of a young anthropologist, A. Terry Rambo, who conducted research in South Vietnam during the mid-1960s. Under a Department of Defense contract and with the cooperation of the South Vietnamese government, Rambo, two other Americans, and a number of Vietnamese university students interviewed thousands of war refugees about their decisions to flee their homes. In the course of the questioning, many of the peasant respondents described how they had been terrorized by the policy of immediate retaliation that had been instituted by South Koreans patrolling their area. The refugees reported that whenever these troops drew fire from a village, they would enter it, line up all the inhabitants, and shoot some at random.

The Vietnamese students were furious. They wanted to return to Saigon immediately and publicly denounce the Koreans for atrocities against unarmed villagers. Rambo believed his method of sampling made it virtually impossible for collusion to have existed among the peasants who detailed these events, and he was convinced of the veracity of the accusations. Yet he persuaded his assistants that it would be more effective to proceed through "proper channels." He felt certain that American military authorities would not sanction such behavior on the part of their allies. Rambo later described his discussions and lengthy briefings with various high-level military officers. They listened politely and with interest. Nonetheless, he was eventually told that no action was contemplated. He was also advised against filing any report about the alleged actions of the Korean troops. Rambo ignored these instructions and wrote a detailed account of his findings for the Department of Defense in Washington. The report itself remained a classified document, and no action has ever been undertaken against any of the Koreans.

Rambo disclosed these events in January 1970, almost four years after he and his associates had conducted their field work.[20] It is apparent that the investigators continue to harbor profound feelings of ambivalence about the entire incident, feelings deeply reinforced by the disclosures of massacres of hundreds of civilians by American troops.

What were the legitimate demands of *personal*, *group*, or *bureaucratic* reciprocity in this instance? What was the researcher's responsibility, and to whom did he owe the greater loyalty? Rambo's painful reflections reveal the nature of his research effort, expose some of the human costs of the longest war this nation has ever fought, and underscore the conflicts that the researcher may face as he attempts to determine where his major obligations lie.

Rambo clearly states the basis for his commitment to American policy in Vietnam. His earlier research in British Honduras and Guatemala had convinced him that the communists had put great pressure on local peasants to gain their support.[21] He was deeply critical of the potential for totalitarian rule that communist organizational ability promised.[22] Like John F. Kennedy and many of his associates, Rambo felt that American policy could allow the South Vietnamese to make their own choice of future governments:

My decision to remain silent and to dissuade my interviewers from public outcry was not made out of any sense of obligation to the United States military as sponsor of my research, but was rather based upon the belief that making a public protest would seriously damage the allied war effort in Vietnam—an effort that I then fully supported although I was already disturbed by many of the effects of this effort on the civilian population.

My written report was filed in Washington with the Office of the Secretary of Defense, which is supposedly a civilian-controlled branch of our government. In reality, of course, the entire United States government administrative apparatus is caught-up in prosecuting the war so that there are no longer distinctions between civil and military roles. This is not, I think, because the military have consciously tried to escape from civilian control but rather because the civilian policy makers have, in effect, voluntarily become militarized. Every responsible United States government officer from President Nixon down to the local unit commanders in Vietnam now has full details on the extent of Korean atrocities, yet nothing effective has been done to stop such activity—but if you had told me back in July 1966 that such would be the case, I would not have believed you.

What was my constituency in Vietnam? The families in Phy-Yen Province who had suffered at the hands of the Koreans? The other million refugees I was supposed to be studying? The Vietnamese government, which was a co-sponsor of my study and which had personnel assigned to working with me in the field who also became involved in decision making on what to do about our findings? The United States government? The American people?

In Vietnam I was not engaged in the study of a tribal village where I was on a first name basis with my informants—I was running a massive survey research project covering large areas of a nation of some sixteen million people, and I was doing it in the middle of one of the most confused wars (in terms of telling who the good guys are) in modern history. I have still not resolved the constituency question and am not sure that there is any right answer— I have a real affection for the Vietnamese as people but I remain an American and there is inevitably a built-in potential for conflict in my role as a researcher in Vietnam.

I know my own sense of guilt over my mishandling of the Korean atrocity data increased in direct proportion to my development of close personal relationships with Vietnamese. In fact I can actually date my final disaffection from official policy considerations to a meal I shared with a group of peasants in the summer of 1969. The "body count" became irrevocably transformed for me into Nguyen and Hanh and Thuy that day—but that occurred after I had lived in a village for some time and had learned a bit of Vietnamese.

In any case my regrets over my handling of the findings on the Koreans stem from a sense of having made a wrong moral choice which, in effect, betrayed all of my possible constituencies (including me, as a person) rather than from a sense of having failed any particular group. Regardless of where my primary loyalties lay or should have lain I was wrong in allowing essentially short-term political considerations to outweigh basic moral issues: I would now argue that reprisal killing of civilians by any force for any reason is unjustifiable (may I use the word "evil"?) and should be opposed by all men, be they scientists or not, in all situations. I realize that my concluding that the ends don't justify the means is about as exciting as another rediscovery of the wheel but I suspect a lot of "committed" social scientists are going to face similar painful discoveries in the future—especially as those students who talk so fondly of the "Third World Peoples" begin to gain direct exposure to the realities of revolutionary action among peasant populations.[23]

Rambo is in an unenviable position. He saw the face of bestiality and turned away because he believed that American military strength could build a better Vietnam. Rambo is guilt-ridden. In his own eyes he is a moral accomplice to United States war crimes in Southeast Asia.

Rambo's initial enthusiasm for the Vietnam War, his sense of exhilaration in carrying a gun and moving into dangerous areas, and his eventual disillusionment were repeated shortly afterward by another American social scientist. Daniel Ellsberg, an economist on the staff of the Rand Corporation, also went to Vietnam convinced that the defeat of the communist-led forces was essential and that social science could lend a strong helping hand. Yet Ellsberg turned from his association with

Pentagon policies to assume an active anti-war position. His experiences in the war zone and the influence of his wife converted him from his long commitment to a hard-line cold war position.

Most important for Ellsberg, the anti-war movement, and the history of the United States in the 1970s, Ellsberg had worked on and had access to a massive 47 volume Pentagon-sponsored history of American involvement in Vietnam. The documents, classified as top secret, detailed the Johnson administration's duplicity in building up American forces on the Asian mainland while publicly espousing a policy in direct opposition to such a momentous move. The American people and the United States Congress itself were provided with a complete version of these and many other decisions taken by the Eisenhower, Kennedy, Johnson, and Nixon administrations when Ellsberg turned the documents over to *The New York Times*.

Ellsberg disappeared for several days after *The New York Times* and several other papers began publishing the material in June 1971. The identity of the man who had leaked the "Pentagon papers" to the *Times* was revealed by a former *Times* reporter and corroborated by Ellsberg himself on the day of his arrest for "stealing government documents."

Ellsberg, who had left Rand so that he could more fully express his anti-war sentiments, had already charged his country with a major responsibility for the death of one to two million Vietnamese over a period of twenty-five years. Like Rambo, he decried an American attitude that defined the Vietnamese as objects to be manipulated. Now, as he surrendered to federal officials, he calmly expressed his belief that the American people had a right to know what its own government had been doing. Ellsberg had clearly rejected any sense of loyalty to the sponsors of the research or to those policies that he felt had resulted in the death of countless Asians and Americans. He stood ready, he said, to accept whatever consequences his act would entail for himself and his family.

The appropriate demands for reciprocity plague many researchers, their sponsors, colleagues, and respondents, as the cases discussed in this section reveal. Whyte was very much concerned about the sensitivities of those who had accepted him into their community and had assisted his investigation.

Some of his respondents raised questions about his portrayal of them and their lives. While Vidich and Bensman seemed content with the results of their research, administrators and researchers at Cornell feared that their book, which was based on data collected while Vidich worked for Cornell, would hurt Springdale and poison its relationship with the university. The military funding for the last two months of my field work undermined my confidence that I had dealt justly with the Chileans and lent credence to the charge that I was really an agent of American intelligence. Berreman admits that the villagers of Sirkanda gained little from his research and demands that all anthropologists reexamine the nature of their scholarly commitment. Rambo continues to suffer with the knowledge that he stood by after unarmed Vietnamese villagers were slaughtered. Ellsberg has acted courageously to expose those who he felt had done irreparable damage to his country but is tortured by whether he should have acted earlier. Placed side by side, these experiences portray an ascending level of agony about the consequences of field research.

# (B)

# reciprocity reconsidered

The dimensions of reciprocity cast a shadow over the entire research adventure. Certainly many researchers complete their efforts satisfied that they have hurt no one intentionally and, indeed, that their work has benefited their hosts. A poll of respondents and informants might elicit a similar evaluation. Yet the instances where a more negative result would occur seem quite frequent. In the quiet of their libraries, many field workers have no doubt pondered what their efforts have added up to. Have they accomplished their goals of understanding and aiding those they have studied or, at least, not inadvertently harmed them?[24]

The questions have become ever more serious and demanding of attention as groups in this country and elsewhere have become increasingly self-conscious about their marginal or exploited position. Many are less willing than ever before to be scrutinized, as Gerald D. Berreman's observations make clear or as the Camelot researchers learned. Respondents and informants are asking more forcefully, "Which side are you on?" Social scientists are debating whether there is a precise answer to this question.

Many younger researchers, often coming out of an activist background themselves, have begun to argue for a committed social science, one that, according to them, is far more sensitive to the kinds of people it studies, the nature of the questions that it poses, and the use to which its findings are put.[25] These researchers argue that social scientists must be wary of continuing to probe the lives of the poor and powerless lest the data be used to control and manipulate those who are already without influence. Some social scientists proclaim that they can no longer afford to maintain the fiction of detachment. Rather, they vehemently argue, researchers must take an active stand in assisting the variety of groups struggling for their own liberation. Committed researchers must put their intellectual skills at the service of the insurgents or fight side by side with them as they attempt to build new institutions.

These social scientists who are so critical of the current direction of their disciplines also stress the importance of refocusing research attention on those who control the multitude of power centers in our society. They know that this is no easy task. Administrators in government, business, and the unions who pass on requests for research funds or who must acquiesce before field workers can study their own organizations are reluctant to assist those who might expose their decisions in an unfavorable light. Furthermore, field workers are not infrequently put under great pressure to modify their interpretations, or to dilute material that some of their influential hosts find distasteful.

I will argue that there is much to be gained from such experiences. The field worker learns how important the support of his colleagues is. He may face the realities of institutional accommodation and the pain of finding that expediency is often more honored than principle. Perhaps most significantly, field workers have to confront one of the most pressing issues of social science research: how to resolve the profound tension between exposure of what is beyond the facade of social conduct and avoidance of harm to those we study? Does this last concern apply only when the field worker is studying people without influence, prestige, or economic resources? Is there another standard when the investigator focuses on decision-makers in government, business, or the professions? There are as yet no final answers to these crucial questions, and the debate rages, as I will make abundantly clear in the following pages.

## STUDYING LOW-INFLUENCE PEOPLE

WHEREIN SOCIAL SCIENTISTS WHO CONSIDER THE CONSEQUENCES
OF THEIR RESEARCH AND WONDER HOW THEY MAY BEST SERVE
BOTH SCHOLARSHIP AND THE NEEDS OF THE UNDERDOG
COME TO DISTINCTLY DIFFERENT CONCLUSIONS.

The sensitive issues of reciprocity that Whyte, Vidich and Bensman, and I faced as we pondered the personal reactions of our respondents, that Berreman and I confronted in the explosive issue of military sponsorship of overseas research, and that Rambo and his colleagues agonized over while assessing their responsibility for the loss of Vietnamese life, all serve as vivid background to the current concerns of other field workers. What legitimate expectations for reciprocity exist when the social scientist gathers data on the lives of low-status respondents that may have important publicity value? What responsibility does the field worker have to prevent his findings from exposing his hosts to ridicule? Is it ever advisable to suppress certain information? And finally, is it now time, as some radical social scientists advocate, to put oneself more actively at the service of the oppressed and exploited in American society and all over the globe?

Lee Rainwater and David J. Pittman have perceptively raised some of these very questions.[26] Their own research focused on a low-income housing project near downtown St. Louis whose residents exhibited many of the characteristics of social breakdown. During the early stages of the so-called War on Poverty, the Social Science Institute of Washington University at St. Louis received a substantial grant from the National Institute of Mental Health to conduct a basic research study of the housing project, which had often been in the news. The grant itself received much local publicity, and a major question of reciprocity soon confronted the researchers. They were deeply concerned with the uses of their findings. The Housing Project study had been defined as basic research, but, as is often the case, the social scientists hoped that their findings would benefit the residents. Rainwater recalled, however, how his earlier research findings on the attitude of lower-class women to the use of birth control had been distorted to mean that the women were uninterested in it. In this instance, he and Pittman feared that their emphasis on lower-class social problems would be interpreted as evidence of the inferiority of these people.

The faculty and graduate students working on the project struggled with the possible distortion of their efforts. They debated what effect their penetrating study of the life styles of the poor would have on the general public. "That is, if one describes in full and honest detail behavior which the public will regard as immoral, degraded, deviant, and criminal, will not the effect be to damage the very people we hope our study will eventually help?"[27]

Other members of the social science fraternity have raised similar points of concern, but from a different perspective. Those who identify with a "radical" sociology charge their colleagues with a deliberate tendency to study the lives of the poor in detail while neglecting those at the top.

Martin Nicolaus has presented a clear critique. He condemns his sociological colleagues for their allegiance to the "establishment," for their defining as social "problems" those actions that disturb society's elite, for "spying" on those subject people, here and abroad, who dream of revolution. To Nicolaus, sociology is simply a tool of the powerful. He caustically asks what the impact would be were social scientists to turn their full attention to the "wealthy and powerful." What if *their* lives

... were daily scrutinized by a thousand systematic researchers, were pried into hourly, analyzed and cross-referenced, tabulated and published in a hundred inexpensive mass circulation journals, and written so that the fifteen-year-old high school drop out could understand it and predict the actions of those who manipulate and control him and thereby resist and overthrow them more effectively?[28]

Social scientists have responded differently to these concerns and accusations. Some have maintained the legitimacy of the scholarly study of the poor and oppressed and have argued that an understanding of their struggles is a central responsibility of social science that can also contribute to an alleviation of this condition. Others have decided that research on the poor must stress those social institutions and beliefs that contribute to the underprivileged position of certain social groups. A third segment of social scientists has determined to put their skills directly at the service of the "underdogs." These investigators maintain that the less powerful desperately need the help of professionals who are competent to interpret American reality to them or who are willing to undertake research into social arrangements that favor the economically wealthy and politically powerful. These social scientists believe that it is not a dearth of studies on the "wealthy and powerful" that is the fundamental problem. They argue, rather, that the available knowledge is simply useless until it is translated into the language of the common man.

The late Oscar Lewis held a unique place among the many social scientists who have studied the life style of the poor in this country and elsewhere. He dedicated his considerable scholarly energies to recording and interpreting the struggles, failures, satisfactions, and joys of those who live within, what he called, the "culture of poverty."[29] Lewis explicitly maintained that it was his scholarly goal to capture the essence of their existence and, where possible, make comparisons across national boundaries. For Oscar Lewis, reciprocity was inherent in the attention, respect, and deep personal and scholarly interest with which he approached his respondents. His books on the Sánchez family in Mexico, the Ríos family in Puerto Rico and New York won him fame, fortune, and condemnation. Many defenders of his approach within and outside of the academic community have found Lewis' material graphic and invaluable. Critics, while applauding his ingenuity in convincing the families to devote hours to the tape recorder, accused Lewis of holding these families up to public ridicule. They maintained that he has placed the great burden for their impoverished and powerless conditions on their own shoulders. From my perspective, Lewis' "culture of poverty" approach, which stresses the significance of the life style of the poor in perpetuating their own poverty, underplays the influence of social institutions in keeping the poor in their socially marginal positions.[30]

Other social scientists, wary of feeding popular prejudices, less sanguine than Oscar Lewis about the significance of simply recording the lives of the poor even in their own words, and

committed to challenging racial inequality, have become increasingly explicit in designing their research to avoid some of
the pitfalls outlined by Rainwater, Pittman, and Nicolaus. The
marked variation in their responses, however, reflects the continuing controversy.

Elliot Liebow, whose study *Tally's Corner* I discussed earlier,
continues to be convinced that economic and political factors
are crucial in the liberation of black people. He recently re-
marked that if he had to rewrite his now famous study, he
would have emphasized that belief even more strongly. Liebow
insists that there is no *one* best way to attempt to help others
and does not accept the view that black workingmen can
achieve their own liberation apart from fundamental change
in public policy. He is also critical of the assertion that groups
simply open themselves up to manipulation from those above
by accepting the overtures of the researcher. On the contrary,
data secured from subjects can help expose both the mechanisms and consequences of exploitation and thereby enhance the
effectiveness of those who are working to change them.

Liebow argues that:

Studying expoited populations is one way for social scientists to achieve the goals of understanding and helping, for
studies may not only contribute to the increased politiciza-
tion and activism of particular persons and groups, but also
these studies may help educate the larger society to its own
destructiveness and to its own responsibility for things that,
historically, it does not even want to look at or think
about.[31]

Liebow does not fear the consequences of honestly writing
about the poor, and his only stipulation for studying a group
is its willingness to cooperate with his research after an honest
explanation as to what he is about. While he respects the right
of any people to decide against cooperation, he vehemently
rejects the legitimacy of fellow social scientists attempting to
direct their colleagues' efforts by labeling them as tools of the
"establishment." Liebow makes a strong case against any form
of censorship.[32]

Michael Lewis, like Liebow a white social scientist, comes to
a somewhat different conclusion from his experiences in learn-

ing about the traps inherent in a unidimensional study of the poor. For his doctoral research in the early 1960s, Michael Lewis decided to focus on the black mother-dominated family in Harlem. He wanted to understand the "dynamics of victimization," the manner by which young blacks were prepared in their earliest family socialization experiences to accept failure in later encounters with crucial marital and economic roles. Lewis read the records of a local welfare agency and interviewed sixty multiproblem families, identified as such by the agency. As he began to analyze the data that focused on the internal dynamics of the families, Lewis realized that his findings could be misinterpreted. As a result, he reevaluated his research design and decided to do a historical analysis of the evolution of black family structures. This analysis revealed the extent to which the black family had adapted to conditions of oppression and societal neglect. Lewis also initiated an historical study of the functioning of the welfare system. His research highlighted the increasingly ineffective role that social work has played in helping the poor as social workers became less politically astute and more interested in developing their professional standing. In essence, as a result of his concern for the possible misuse of his work, Michael Lewis had refocused his intellectual outlook and developed what I would maintain is a more sophisticated approach, one to which I would subscribe.

Michael Lewis' later study of the black community in a Midwestern city is a direct outgrowth of these research experiences. Working with several associates and a large staff, and willing to commit several years to the investigation, Lewis applied the "competence" model that he formulated from his earlier study. The research team studied the impact of family, neighborhood, social agencies, schools, courts, and the white power structure in the development of competence skills and attitudes by young blacks. The report stressed the influence and responsibility of white-dominated institutions on the black community.[33]

Michael Lewis expresses deep concern about blacks and other exploited groups. He is also ardently committed to scholarship. Like Liebow, he has not despaired about influencing important government officials, and his report has been sent to a variety of national and local leaders. But Lewis argues that this is not sufficient. Social scientists, he believes, must actively seek out those groups struggling for social change. Scholarly sophistication can and should arm these people. Lewis is now advocating the importance of direct service to the oppressed.[34]

Lewis does not talk of discarding his scholarly values. He believes his best contribution can be made by a continuing commitment to hard-nosed analysis. For him, the crucial question is exactly how the dedicated social scientist may contribute both to an understanding of social processes and to social justice. Lewis and others are not unaware of the awesome tensions that are inherent in pursuing both ends. Yet, they are not satisfied that they are now making their best contribution. Commitment to maintaining the integrity of scholarly concerns must, for them, be coupled with directly helping those facing overwhelming odds in their daily struggle for dignity.

How can this be accomplished? I believe the social scientist must, first of all, be deeply sensitive to the extent to which *bureaucratic* reciprocity influences the direction of research. Those who have funds to support research can more easily encourage the investigator to phrase questions from a particular perspective. Marc Pilisuk furnishes us with a recent illustration involving the evaluation of the Head Start Program. The investigators, working with a grant from the Office of Economic Opportunity, spoke at length to the program's designers and implementors. They analyzed documents setting forth goals and measured such factors as reading scores to determine the nature of the children's progress. The findings questioned the effectiveness of the program, and the study was successfully used by those arguing for a cutback in funds.

The investigators, according to Pilisuk, had fallen into traditional traps. They developed their design and yardsticks by drawing upon the impressions and views of their colleagues, the sponsors of the research, and newspaper and journal articles:

By and large, we have used our clinical and intuitive skills to obtain an *understanding* of people who range from our colleagues to our superiors in the Establishment. I would like to suggest that this procedure may on several counts be wrong, that we should perhaps be using our clinical and intuitive skills to listen carefully to what disadvantaged people are saying, to gaining an understanding of their needs and desires, and to direct our more rigorous research efforts to the prediction and control of those people among our colleagues and superiors whose decisions and practices are in large measure responsible for the distress of those whom we have been traditionally studying. Had there been an adequate understanding of what children in the Head Start programs and their parents wanted and were getting from these programs, the question of reading readiness skills may not have been a fundamental one.[35]

Pilisuk then briefly describes his experience with a study of community power holders. He, several colleagues, and graduate students, working with no sponsor's funds, visited the local ghetto. They wanted to understand the types of questions its residents had about the city's power structure. The researchers' explicit goal in this project was to identify decision-makers to those whose lives were shaped by some distant, unreachable "system."

This increasingly important effort is not without its peculiar challenges. Social scientists hoping to assist the poor may often find their efforts resisted by those who claim to speak for the oppressed and who are thus deeply suspicious of "outside" help. In the late 1960s, Henry A. Landsberger, a sociologist with long experience in Latin America, decided to follow up his study of peasant movements there by analyzing black farmer cooperatives in the United States South. Landsberger felt that the problems of discrimination, exploitation, and violence against the poor were likely to be similar in both regions, and he wanted to bring his experience to bear on the struggle of southern blacks. Landsberger, working as a Ford Foundation consultant, won cordial acceptance from the indigenous farm leaders who made up the Board of Directors of the Federation of Southern Cooperatives, as well as from the members of the individual black farmers' co-ops and their officers. But he quickly learned that the middle-class executives who administered the federation were less than happy with his presence. Despite several directives from the board, Landsberger never received the cooperation of his youthful, often urban-born, more highly educated, and certainly more radical critics. These men, who included several whites as well as blacks, wanted Ford Foundation funds but resisted an independent evaluation of their efforts. Landsberger, a seasoned and tough veteran of intra-organizational conflict, pursued his research nonetheless and proposed some rather novel suggestions to improve the coopera-tives' functioning.

Most important for this discussion, however, are Lands-berger's unwillingness to retreat under pressure from militants who claim to speak for the poor, his incisive analysis of the manner in which well-meaning foundation personnel can be led to soft-pedal issues in order to maintain the support of those they are trying to study and help, and perhaps most crucial, his hard-bitten assertion that knowledge is essential for libera-tion. If social scientists are really on the side of the poor, Lands-berger cogently argues, they must stand ready to be the bearer of unpleasant truths:

To query the feasibility of a project for the poor or the black on any basis except that it is really "an establish-ment plot to avoid tackling the underlying problem," is to lay oneself open to charges of racism, insensitivity, and the like. But to query a project on such specific bases as the possible lack within the poor or black communities of tech-nical or managerial skills; or to conclude that membership apathy is a fact of life among poor blacks (*as it is among poor and rich whites*) is to make certain that such accusa-tions will be made. As in the case of charges of communist sympathies, such accusations are difficult to refute, cer-tainly at an early enough point. An aura of suspicion tends to adhere. Since all of this is very unpleasant personally and in addition also has the practical effect of lessening one's acceptability (and hence one's future utility and hence one's future funding), few people are willing to speak out.

Mercifully, I can indeed be frank, not at all because I am more virtuous than others, but because my style of work happens to be one which is less dependent on the support of others, financial and otherwise. I have never conducted research based on large grants and probably never will. In any case, I think well enough of my fellow man—both the humble in the co-ops, and the powerful in the founda-tions and in the government—to believe that they fre-quently, and increasingly, welcome the truth.[36]

Howard S. Becker and Steven Dedijer have also made some specific and highly pertinent observations for those interested in *Counter-Establishment R & D*.[37] They argue that researchers concerned about the power of the various establishments in this country and elsewhere should spend more effort ingeniously seeking out funds and time through which to pursue their work and expend less effort in complaining about their impotence. Some concrete suggestions are put forth toward this end. Thus, for example, social scientists critical of current political, economic, social, or moral establishments could convince government to support their work with the argument that critics might come up with some better alternative or, at least, insist it is important to know what critical men and women are up to. Universities could be pressured toward providing some small percentage of their funds to support such research. Private foundations and patrons could be convinced that the severity of the problem necessitates some unorthodox investigations.

Should all these attempts fail, anti-establishment investigators could try far less expensive methods of data collection by drawing upon available personnel. The history of social science field work, I would stress, is replete with examples of excellent insight contributed by local informants. Many of these people have already been cited in early pages of this volume. Others like them could be trained. Indeed, the committed researcher of group life might make his most profound and most radical contribution by assisting indigenous personnel in working up their own studies. Not only information but also useful skills would remain long after the researcher had gone on to other work.

Perhaps Becker and Dedijer's most forceful argument is their last. They flatly assert that it is important to know. Arguments that scientific knowledge is used only for repressive ends or, conversely, that it is seldom relevant must not paralyze researchers.[38] If someone is interested in revolution, for example, it may be very important to understand the process whereby political energies of rebels are worn thin by continual factionalism. History has proved that ideological rhetoric is simply no substitute for clear-headed and careful analysis on this and many other issues.[39]

Becker and Dedijer end their discussion by emphasizing the

importance of diversity in scholarly approach and commitment. Their paper continues the useful consideration of the ways in which such diversity may be achieved by researchers increasingly unhappy about the contribution of social science to the solution of major social issues.

These suggestions, I must observe, are not without danger to those who would take them seriously. Laud Humphreys considers himself in strong agreement with Becker's approach to sociological research, as his study of impersonal sex reveals.[40] Humphreys has long maintained that homosexuals have been unduly persecuted by the forces of social control in a morally repressive society. His research, which used government funds, was directed toward carefully testing this assertion. Humphreys was not only content to publish his findings, which argue for an end to police harassment and blackmail and the repeal of legal sanctions, but has also *joined* the struggle toward that end:

Beginning in the Spring of 1969, my wife and I helped found the Mandrake Society, a homophile organization in St. Louis. A number of my actual respondents became active in this group. Late that year, in connection with research I was conducting in Boston, I began working with a small group of interested individuals to develop the Homophile Union of Boston. These two groups now have hundreds of members. Since our arrival in Albany, we have helped in the development of the Tri-Cities Gay Liberation Front. I have been elected to the Board of the North American Conference of Homophile Organizations and helped found the Council for Sexual Civil Liberties.

To my mind, such activity, at my own expense, is simply part of the essential reciprocity that must obtain between the social scientist and his "less powerful" research subjects. If those he studies cry out for liberation, he must help with that liberation—and on their terms. This conviction, I suspect, is reflected in my work; and that may explain why the most favorable reviews of *Tearoom Trade* have appeared in homophile publications.

The research adventure has led me to "tell it like it is," and groups low on the American power scale appreciate the exposure of their conditions, in proportion to the fidelity of the resulting report.[41]

Yet, others were far less enthusiastic about Humphreys' research and his advocacy of the rights of homosexuals. In May 1970, Humphreys and several hundred faculty and students at the University of Southern Illinois were involved in a demonstration against the invasion of Cambodia by United States and South Vietnamese troops. According to Humphreys, he helped avoid a potentially explosive situation by leading the student demonstrators off campus and into the local selective service office. Once there, he tore a picture of President Nixon, again hoping that this symbolic act of protest would cool the tempers of the outraged critics of administration policy. Humphreys believes that because of his efforts there was no violence in Edwardsville that day.

However, he was arrested a short time later by the F.B.I. and charged with the felony of interfering with the administration of the Selective Service Act and the misdemeanor of destroying a picture of President Nixon. Humphreys eventually pleaded guilty to the lesser charge and was sentenced to four months in federal prison, with eight more months suspended sentence and three years of probation. Humphreys is now appealing what he and his attorneys consider to be a harsh sentence. Howard S. Becker and James Short served as co-chairmen of the Humphreys Defense Committee and helped raise funds to defray a great portion of the lawyers' fees.

Humphreys is convinced that the nature of his research and defense of homosexuals were prime factors in his arrest and sentence. It is extremely difficult to weigh the various factors involved, as Humphreys himself states, but he can cite some interesting evidence in support of his assertion. He relates that the arresting officers seemed to know a great deal about his research and talked about nothing else:

F.B.I. agents en route to my booking spoke very knowledgeably of my research. They knew at least what the newspapers had said of the "furor" at Washington University. They were thoroughly familiar with the *Transaction* excerpt; and at least one had read my book. They talked quite frankly about the study; e.g., did I really believe there was no danger to teenagers? They presumed the locale was St. Louis, but I emphasized that I surveyed the situation in nine cities. To stop them from pumping me, I held forth on the four types of homosexuals described in the [*Trans-*

*action*] article. One man said he had intended to take some courses from me at S.I.U. Other than this, they talked about nothing else during those twenty minutes.[42]

Humphreys was later told by informants that the F.B.I. has an "immense file" on him, that he has been under military surveillance, and that his phone has been tapped. While, again, there is no hard evidence for these statements, it is apparent that the authorities have some source of information about Humphreys' activities and statements even within his own classroom:

The probation officer here who interviewed me as part of my pre-sentencing investigation read back to me out-of-context quotations from my lectures at Albany as well as at Southern Illinois University. Primarily, these had to do with remarks I had made about J. Edgar Hoover. I simply assured him that I thought Hoover to be the best friend the criminal had in America—and that John Mitchell might run a close second—and let it go at that. This interrogation lasted four hours and was one of the most thoroughly demoralizing experiences of my lifetime. Largely, it was shattering because it made me distrust my students.[43]

Recent revelations about the extent of military surveillance of even the most respectable citizens bear witness to Humphreys' statements. Members of the United States Senate have become irate by the routine dossiers that are kept on prominent persons, including senators, involved in civil rights and anti-war activities.[44] For Humphreys, any surveillance has particularly negative professional consequences:

During the hearings on motions prior to my trial, the F.B.I. denied that they had any employees assigned to me but refused to speak for other agencies. These things don't bug me as they did at first. I simply take for granted now that everything I say and do goes on record in some agency or other. The problem with field research is more serious, however. I have enough reason to believe I am under surveillance that I dare not risk the strong possibility of incriminating respondents. I can speak only at homophile

meetings and interview leaders—because they have proclaimed their homosexuality by their involvement in the
movement.

The second problem was suggested by a couple of my
colleagues who are police experts. They came to my office
one day to tell me that they had good reason to believe the
F.B.I. routinely notifies the police of every community I
visit. This, they cautioned, poses a physical danger to me.
The F.B.I. is just professional enough not to pose a physical
threat. When local departments receive a description of
"Criminal No. 7002 (that is my number), convicted of destroying government property in a draft board demonstration, engaging in research with sexual deviants," that is
taken as an open invitation for the local boys in blue to set
a trap that might excuse their arresting me on some charge
or beating the shit out of me. These colleagues begged me
to stay out of the field "for the duration."

The conditions of the excessive sentence, pronounced
after I had pleaded guilty to the misdemeanor of destroying the President's picture, were, I believe, specifically
designed to preclude further research in deviant behavior
on my part. Four months in a federal prison is unusually
severe for a first offense where the destroyed property was
worth, perhaps, a dollar. But the three years of probation
imposed, with its condition that "you shall associate only
with law-abiding persons and maintain reasonable hours,"
means that the sort of research in which I am proficient
is terminated. Unless my appeal is successful, I shall be
forty-five and out of contact by the time I finish paying for
my crime of diverting students from violence on my
campus and in the nearby community.

Not only have those in political power denounced the
Commission on Pornography, because it violated expectations, but they have taken unusual steps to prevent research that exposes the sexual substructure of the society.
People have often wondered if I didn't feel threatened by
my respondents. Not at all! That relationship, I trust, will
continue to be mutually rewarding. But God help social
scientists as they respond to the challenge of Martin
Nicolaus. Beware the violation of reciprocity with the
"wealthy and powerful"—whether they are the subjects of
research or not.

Experts in constitutional law assure me that the authors of the "Bill of Rights" were not really concerned about the violations of privacy that, of necessity, occur always at the hands of probing neighbors, salesmen, journalists, and social scientists. We are inventive creatures and have a grand array of mechanisms with which to defend ourselves against such prying. The real concern of the founders of our liberties was with protecting the citizen against the awful force of military and social control agencies, who have the power to arrest, prosecute, imprison, and destroy those whose privacy they violate. As I wrote Nicholas von Hoffman shortly after my arrest: "You see, the real point is that the former [John Mitchell *et al.*] can and do arrest the latter [Laud Humphreys *et al.*]."[45]

Humphreys has vehemently defended himself against accusations that his research is mere pornography, that he has been unethical in his data collection procedures, and that he deserves to be put in prison for his anti-war activities. On the contrary, he defines himself as an ally of the underdog, as someone more concerned with peace and nonviolence than his own safety.

Humphreys rejects the arguments of some of his colleagues that the social sciences study the less powerful simply because they are more available and less resistant. Rather, he argues, field workers are normally attracted to study those with whom they sympathize. When such feeling is combined with a commitment to fight for those groups unjustly condemned by the larger society, the researcher has fulfilled his duty.

The controversy about whether or not to study the poor, underprivileged, and weak will continue.[46] Some field workers will write insightfully about these people while hoping that their observations and words have a positive impact on the lives of their hosts. A few like Humphreys will go far beyond study and become frontline activists in the struggle for their respondents' liberation. The fate of these field workers will continue to be an important indication of the health of American society. Other social scientists will act upon their convictions by actually attempting research on the powerful.[47] These investigators will no doubt learn as they enter that less well-marked terrain that the prospects and problems of field research have some peculiar contours there.

## STUDYING HIGH-INFLUENCE PEOPLE

WHEREIN SOCIAL SCIENTISTS CONFRONT THOSE WITH POWER
AND LEARN ABOUT THE KINDS OF PRESSURES THAT CAN BE PLACED
UPON FIELD WORKERS AND THEIR SUPERIORS.

Studying people with influence can present an unusual challenge. Vidich and Bensman came under a heavy barrage of
criticism from hosts who read their material and who were
able to make their views known to the other Cornell researchers associated with the project. The writers were flayed for
abuse of hospitality and for the critical picture they drew of
certain aspects of life in Springdale. Vidich and Bensman successfully resisted any attempt to modify their report because
they were beyond the influence of both Springdale *and* Cornell.
Other researchers have proved more vulnerable. Jane Cassels
Record has aptly described the unique pressures to which university research institutes and their staffs are especially subject.[48]
Since much of social science research now occurs under institute auspices, the cases she describes are important in discussing the problems of *bureaucratic* reciprocity when studying
the influential. Her report further indicates the range of clients
who may be offended by critical accounts of themselves or of
their organizations.

Record first discusses a study that examined the role of
labor union business agents. The investigation was conducted by
a mature graduate student, who reported quite favorably on the
functioning of the union. His manuscript, however, contained
one chapter that raised serious questions concerning the degree
of power wielded by the business agent. Although he performed
his duties efficiently, the concentration of power in his hands,
the researcher observed, raised serious questions about the
future of union democracy.

In accordance with their previously arranged understanding,
the union's business agent was permitted by the institute's
director to read the completed report. The official vehemently
objected to the chapter that raised the sensitive issue of power
and democracy. An officer of the national union, who served on

the institute's board, quickly contacted the director. He emphasized that the business agent was effective, efficient, and strongly supported by his members. The controversial chapter raised issues that would harm the local. The institute's director approached the young investigator about the possibility of excluding the chapter from the published report. He received a firm negative reply and finally discussed the problem with his executive council. These senior associates, while agreeing to the importance of the freedom of publication, asserted that the controversial chapter might better be included in a comparative study of internal union democracy and they postponed publication of the findings. That second investigation, Record concludes, has yet to be initiated.

A similar instance of client pressure also occurred in a study of union management relations. A young researcher, working at a state university, critically evaluated the nature of the negotiation process. He felt that the union in one case had gained less favorable working conditions than had been obtained in comparable industries. Both management and labor condemned these findings as unfounded, and a management representative threatened to appeal to high-level state political leaders if publication ensued. The institute's director placated the management representative by assuring him that the manuscript needed to undergo extensive revision. Publication would not occur without further consultation with all involved parties.

A third case reported by Record dealt with the relationship between the federal government and an institute of a small private university. The government agency offered to make a very substantial grant available to the new and struggling institute if it would pursue a particular research problem. The institute director contacted two university sociologists who were working in the very area under consideration. At a meeting with the government representatives, these men argued that the research focus be broadened to include a wider range of pertinent material. The representatives steadfastly refused until it became apparent that they feared that the recommendations would result in an investigation of politically sensitive material. Other social scientists from the institute later argued against continuing the negotiations. They felt that the government was intent on specifying the limits of the efforts, and they sensed that there would be an attempt to censor the findings. The research director of the institute decided to proceed over their objections. His goal was to develop the institute into a viable research oraganization, and the federal funds were simply too tempting.

These three cases illustrate some of the difficulties that may face the social scientist when he is associated with an institute. When that institute is subject to political and financial pressure, the researcher is in a vulnerable position. He may quickly learn that the institute is not only concerned with the integrity of his individual effort, but also must consider how the particular incident will affect the long-term interests of the organization. Will a critical account make other groups wary of cooperating with requests for access to conduct research? Will the institute gain the reputation for overzealous debunking of respectable institutions? In sum, the institute is concerned with maintaining good relations with a variety of audiences. It often balances out competing external demands against the needs of one of its staff members.

The institute director is both an administrator and social scientist. Unlike the investigator, his commitment is not only to the publication of research findings. He also asks how this will affect the overall goals of the organization for which he is responsible. At times, Record asserted, his decision will be the one that avoids a head-on confrontation and that refuses to define each crossroad as a matter of vital principle. The institute director learns how to compromise, to see things in terms of grays and not as black or white. For him, there are so many projects to be pursued, so many ways to present a sensitive finding. His view of the ethics of research may be quite different from that of some of his staff members; he faces different problems and different temptations.

Access to a large-scale organization necessitates the cooperation of sophisticated administrators. Many are knowledgeable about social science research and are wary about the impact on their organization of the investigator's findings. They are not willing to open their doors to any and all academics seeking "dispassionately" to contribute to their field's development. They want assurances that the data will not be detrimental to their major objective, the operation and competitive advantage of their organizations. Record observes that social science administrators quickly become aware of the sensitivities of their counterparts in other organizations. In consequence, subtle adjustments may be made in the research design and in the agreements about reviewing the findings.

The crucial observation for our purposes concerns the complex nature of the many kinds of reciprocal relationships that develop in the research process. They go beyond personal and group loyalties, which we have previously stressed, and enter the realm of institutional accommodation. As part of his professional socialization process, the young social scientist quickly becomes aware of these realities. If he is unfortunate, he learns by bitter experience that there exist more and less controversial issues, that there are more and less vulnerable research areas, that there are more and less influential respondents and informants.

I was personally involved in a situation somewhat comparable to those discussed by Record, but whose outcome was quite different. In the late 1950s the director of a prominent research institute at a major private university approached the administration of a large nearby industrial laboratory. He requested permission for one of his social science associates to conduct a study of its organization. The study was to analyze the manner in which the laboratory utilized its highly trained scientific personnel. How were they recruited, how were they organized, how did leadership arise, how did they respond to management directives, and how did they keep contact with their colleagues in academia and at other industrial laboratories? In essence, the investigation was to focus on the relationship between management, with its primary concern for the interests of the parent corporation, and the scientists, many of whom were primarily committed to contributing to the development of scientific knowledge and the furtherance of the scientific community as a whole.[49]

It was readily apparent to the laboratory administrators that the request entailed submitting their organization to investigation by social scientists who might delve into sensitive areas. It was also clear, on the other hand, that the academic administrator and his institute were associated with a prestigious university, that they had conducted similar investigations over a period of many years, and that they were not hostile to business interests. The study was part of a larger project that would include subsequent research on a university science department and a large-scale government laboratory. The industrial laboratory's cooperation would facilitate an important comparative study of the organization of scientific research. To show its good faith, the academic institute later agreed to interrupt its research and study the engineering unit of the corporation where a series of internal problems had arisen. This study was far less central to the institute's interest and had less inherent social science relevancy, but it was of deep interest to corporate management.

The actual laboratory study continued about a year later with the full and enthusiastic cooperation of its administration. It had welcomed the engineering study and believed the findings contributed to the well-being of its entire and extensive operations. The laboratory administration gave the investigator and his assistants complete access to the scientific and technical staff and even offered to provide for the typing of the interviews. The last offer, of course, was politely refused.

The industrial scientists, to a man, were cordial to the researchers. They freely reported on the factors that led them to pursue a scientific career, described their graduate school experiences, recalled their decision to accept an industrial versus an academic position, analyzed the process by which they chose a research problem, and explored the satisfactions and strains that they experienced in their research efforts. They freely commented on the advantages and disadvantages of their industrial position and compared themselves to their colleagues in the university.

After a year of interviewing, the report was prepared and submitted in final form to the members of the laboratory administration for comment. Several top management officials responded heatedly to those sections that were most critical of the extent to which the administration understood the special needs of scientific employees. The director of the social science institute and the senior investigator were willing to modify any factual errors, but they steadfastly and successfully refused to change the presentation of interview data or to revise critical statements that appeared as part of the interpretation of the material.

The situation differed in several respects from those described by Record. The academic research institute was part of a prestigious university, committed to serious, scholarly work in its field of interest. The institute had sound financial backing, and it was, therefore, in a secure position to resist pressure from a powerful corporation.

The laboratory administrators, on the other hand, felt stung. They had actively cooperated with the research and had made their facilities and personnel available. Now they felt betrayed by certain sections of the report, for some believed that competing laboratory representatives would exhibit copies of the book to prospective scientific employees. Furthermore, the investigator had distributed the published report to all the scientists interviewed and sections critical of management had been particularly applauded. The administrators feared that the report would become a weapon in scientist-management disputes.[50]

In actuality, the study had illuminated some of the dangers of cooperating with a social science research effort. The administrators thought they completely understood the structure and functioning of their own laboratory. Many had themselves been scientists, and, while they now generally identified with the goals of the corporation, they felt they understood the needs of scientific personnel. They were insufficiently sensitive, however, to the ongoing tensions inherent in the role of industrial scientist. They were not totally cognizant of the problems that confronted a young scientist who had been trained in a university department and who now found himself in a substantially different organizational milieu. They failed to appreciate fully the problem of response to authority that troubles an experienced scientist, committed to basic research, who has his work evaluated partly in terms of its contribution to the corporate profit structure. They lacked a full identification with the tensions and uncertainty of scientific research.

Perhaps, most fatally, they did not appreciate that the social scientist had little loyalty to management. His obligation to them was markedly tempered by his explicit commitment to examine all weaknesses in internal laboratory relationships and by his own identification with the scientists. Arlene Kaplan Daniels, whose work I discussed earlier, has captured the essence of this situation in dramatic fashion:

...the conviction has grown upon me that inviting researchers into an organization is equivalent to the sorcerer in fantasy tales who calls up the demons and permits them to enter the charmed circle. Once invoked, demons have a logic and a direction of their own. The moral in such tales is that one is supposed to consider this aspect of the matter before the invoking. To the extent, then, that sociologists have a calling or a perspective of their own, they have the responsibility to follow it in whatever situation they conduct research. If the researchers' affiliations and interests become so closely allied with the organization studied that they cannot view it in any disparaging light without severe discomfort, they are in danger of changing professions—becoming organizers, lobbyists, personnel officers, or some other kind of official responsible to the organization. The organization also has a choice—either to close itself off from access to researchers who might view its processes in a disparaging light, or to resign itself to the possibility that research findings may be both useful and discomfiting. The situation is felt most keenly on both sides, I believe, when the organization is supporting the researcher. In my case, I was often made to feel "how sharper than a serpent's tooth a thankless researcher ... whom we have been supporting in high style." My alternative was to answer: "If you don't like it, don't pay for it ... and I will take the consequences."[51]

The study of the industrial laboratory brings into sharp focus the serious questions Record raised earlier. Much social science research is now being conducted by teams of researchers in large university institutions. Their work often necessitates substantial funding, the agreement of the institute director or board, and, finally, the cooperation of powerful clients. The problem of pressure from a variety of sources is serious. Social science research demands courage and commitment to the belief that our work is vital in the maintenance of a viable, open society. There can be no sacred topics, no areas too sensitive for critical probing. This commitment may be learned and reinforced in the graduate school experience, or it can be undermined by the students' exposure to shades of compromise and expedient scholarship.

The commitment is also reinforced by the daily realities of our work life. Will senior colleagues stand in defense of the right to pursue research freely? Indeed, do they approach their own work in a manner that encourages unfettered research? Do our professional associations act forcefully to minimize unwarranted restraints on free investigation? In essence, is there a spirited attempt to reduce the limitations on scholarly research? Are illegitimate demands for reciprocity resisted?

There is no available census by which we can answer these questions. The pressures on field workers, no doubt, often lead to important revisions in their work. Many of these instances probably go unreported by researchers who prefer to compromise rather than brook the fury of influential sponsors and respondents. A conscious attempt to compile cases of *bureaucratic* intrusion would be enlightening and would serve to alert other social scientists to the variety of dangers they face as they attempt to study those whose power far exceeds their own. Such a file might also arm and embolden field workers who would then be privy to the process whereby such pressure is employed. As is often the case, publicity and lively discussion among colleagues can be of immeasurable help in maintaining commitment to a courageous pursuit of understanding.

The expression of these views does not minimize the importance that must be attached to the rights of influential respondents. It is not only the poor and disadvantaged who should expect consideration from the investigator. As stated earlier, respect for confidentiality and protection of the identities of those studied are legitimate forms of reciprocity. Where research findings can undermine the position of those in authority, as in the laboratory study discussed above, the researcher has entered another realm. In that situation, the social scientists took a forthright position on the importance of presenting a hard-hitting account. Few of their colleagues would have criticized them or would have suggested any other path.

Those in power, whether in public or private positions, have been defined as fair game by social scientists. This is as it should be. Their position often includes the expectation of accountability. Social scientists, among others, have and should continue to strive to ensure that those who control vast administrative organizations are not shielded from the appropriate limelight. Events of the last few years in this country and elsewhere make this more important and more difficult than ever before.

Willard Gaylin's experiences in pursuing his powerful and important research on imprisoned war resisters fuses the many issues raised in this section.[52] Gaylin, a psychoanalyst, hoped to understand the young men who refused induction in protest against the Vietnam War. He first needed the permission and cooperation of prison authorities. The penal bureaucracy's favorable response to his request and its later decision to *exclude* him reveal both the continuing potential for significant research and the retaliatory power that rests in the hands of government bureaucrats. Gaylin recently reflected:

There was a real question in my mind from the beginning why the government would allow me to do work such as this. It was a politically volatile area, they had no real way of knowing me. On the other hand, I was a respectable researcher from a legitimate university, and I do think there is a pressure on any government which pretends to an open mind and pretends to have a respect for research to allow you in. I think not to allow you in indicates a defensiveness and implies they have something to hide. Of course in an area like the prison they always have the rationalization of security to keep you out. They were concerned about this but I later found out it was probably another reason which concerned them—they had a problem, they were frightened, and I looked like someone who might be helpful to them. They thought they could exploit me for their purposes and, indeed, had they asked me to consider the problem, I would have been willing to go along since ultimately it would also benefit the conscientious objectors.

If even 10 percent of the boys who were threatening to go to jail rather than service did go to jail, the government would have a dilemma of where to put them. There are only a certain number of minimum security camps. Once they filled these, they would have had the choice of either sending the resisters to a maximum security prison or creating some special camps for them. If they sent them into maximum security prisons almost assuredly (on a statistical basis) some of them would get severely injured and perhaps killed. These are now middle-class boys, not the usual constituency of a jail, and middle-class boys have access to important people—people with influence in Congress and people with access to the media. The last thing in the world the government wanted, therefore, was adverse publicity.

Take the Berrigan case. There is no question in my mind that when they were first admitted, the government would have gladly, if there were a face-saving way of doing it, spent the $30,000 to send them to some monastery in the south of France to keep their mouths shut. The fact is, that when you have a lot of skeletons in the closest, the last thing you want to do is introduce a light into that closet. A middle-class boy, associated with the peace movement, has connections and is, indeed, a light on in the closet. A charismatic Catholic priest is, of course, a beacon. So the government was not anxious for a couple of reasons to send boys to maximum security prisons. On the other hand, if they send them to a work camp created especially for them, they are in hot water on two counts. The problems in World War II came precisely because political prisoners were segregated. This gave them a chance to pull themselves together as a unit, to form themselves into a political group. In addition it would have the prison authorities open to the accusation that they were setting up political concentration camps—which is indeed what they would look like.[53]

Gaylin's research used the nondirective psychoanalytical interview. The resisters, desperate for someone to talk to, soon came to trust him. The researcher's calm, confident, and warm personal bearing provided the men with acceptance and understanding rare in prison life.

Gaylin learned a great deal about the men, their motivations for refusing to serve, their relationships with parents and prison peers, and their hopes for the future. Gaylin's frequent visits at two federal penitentiaries confronted him with the debilitating impact of prison life. The fear of homosexual attack, the sense of isolation and being forgotten, the subservience to ubiquitous authority destroyed the men's confidence. The prison experience inflicted severe punishment and provided little by way of rehabilitation for the peace prisoners.

In his preliminary manuscript, Gaylin criticized prison life and the unpredictable nature of the parole system. His observations were not received kindly by his hosts and they acted to exclude him from further access to the men. The bureaucrats had obviously not expected that the respected psychiatrist would turn his sights on them:

The expulsion from the prison is extremely important. I had agreed to let them have advance notice before I published anything. I think this is common courtesy. I let them know that I did not give them right of censorship but I would submit manuscripts so that they could correct either any misstatements of fact or any errors of interpretation that they thought were there. When I got the galleys of my book for correction I sent them on to them, requesting their comments. I got no comment except that it was received.

I had arranged for one of my usual trips to the prison. Traditionally I followed this method: I would send a list of the names of the prisoners I was to see with the hours that I wanted to see them to the secretary to the warden. This was usually done on a holiday as those were the only days I could get away from New York and my teaching assignments. On New Year's Day I had planned to be in Lewisburg. The day before I received a call from the warden notifying me that I would not be admitted to the prisons since my research was over. I asked him what gave him that idea. He said he had been told that my book was completed. I explained that the book was not the research but only a part of the research and that was a decision that only the chief researcher—myself—could make. He said he was not about to argue with me; that his decision was final and if I wasn't satisfied, I could call Washington. That was a direct tip-off. Normally, the warden is intimidated by the concept of calling Washington—so it suggested immediately that he had already cleared it or that he had received orders from Washington.

I called Washington and talked to the associate director of prisons. What I did not know at that time, and what might have altered my entire procedure, was that the Director of the Bureau of Prisons, Merle Alexander, a good person, had resigned. The bureau was waiting for a new appointment and was in an interim phase with only an acting director. The associate director told me that as far as he was concerned, with the completion of the book, my research was over. He used the glib excuse, "Everything has to come to an end." I explained very carefully that in a statistical research you endanger years of work if you are not allowed to complete your population (I knew this was not exactly the case for me but certainly any sociological researcher can envision such a phenomenon, and, indeed, it was distressing to be told this—if only as a matter of principle and precedent). I suggested we had a contractual arrangement; that I had told them in advance precisely how long I wanted to work—that is, to follow one day's population of prisoners until every one of the men in my population had been discharged.

I explained too that a precedent was being established which was somewhat dangerous; that he must see the unethical nature of a government granting research (and I allowed that they did not have to grant that) and then on the basis of the direction of the analysis deciding whether the research would be concluded or not. This then becomes censorship and thought control. If the government approved a research plan and then only allowed completion of that research which seemed to prove those things they wanted to prove, and violated or interrupted those researchers which tended to lead in a direction that was threatening to them, this becomes a way of manipulating social scientists. Certainly, it had serious implications since much research must be done within government agencies. No better example can be seen than the whole nature of imprisonment and what it does to men.

He was adamant, was interested in no conclusions, and said if I didn't like it I could make a case of it. At that point I consulted a lawyer and was about to do just that— make a case of it. Then I realized I would have to report the Bureau of Prisons to its immediate superior—the Attorney General of the United States—John Mitchell. It was easy to conceive of Mitchell using any excuse, even if he were not sympathetic to the complaints, to embarrass Merle Alexander (being ignorant at that time of his resignation). I chose, therefore, not to carry the issue ahead, although at this point, I think it might have been a fight worth making.

The callousness of the prisons is such that there was no way I could reach the two boys who were still in prison to explain my abandonment of them (no official way). I was not an authorized correspondent. I could not write to them. No one in the Bureau of Prisons would send a message to explain why I wasn't there. For all practical purposes these men merely thought that I had forgotten about them. I might say that I found illegal, unofficial ways of getting messages to them. This is never a problem in prison. There is something about the prison system which encourages deception and deceit. There is such an abundance of rules that I could never find one of them that was not violated.[54]

Gaylin's research is not over, nor have the prison and judicial authorities heard the last of him. His book has already had and will no doubt continue to have an impact on the future thinking about this painful period in American history. The treatment of those young men who followed their conscience behind prison walls is now well documented. Gaylin's writing and lectures currently inform concerned citizens about those young men still in jail and serve to indict the entire American prison system. Gaylin, in addition, is now turning his attention to men and women who judge, sentence, and review the cases of those who break laws and are brought to justice in this country. The development of Gaylin's research interests over the past few years is a prime example of an investigator first studying the victim and later more directly analyzing the system itself and those who control it:

I had, indeed, anticipated in the second phase of this research going to Canada and studying the war resisters there to see if they were essentially a different population. My reason for changing was quite simple. I had gone to the prisons to study the war resister. Instead, what happened was that *the war resister became a vehicle for my studying the prisons.* I felt that even this war was ultimately going to come to an end but prisons were an institution of the government that would be with us forever and I was horrified at the implications that this might have—or already was having. The sentencing without right to review is a particular horror in the federal courts and has been known to be such for years. I therefore decided to study the nature of bias as it was introduced into the judge's sentencing procedure.[55]

Gaylin is a man of great professional competence. It is apparent to those who have read his book or have listened to his lectures that he is also a person who is deeply concerned about the well-being of men and women behind prison walls. In his efforts, Gaylin symbolizes much that is courageous and dedicated in American scholarship. His work and life reveal that it is possible and, indeed, desirable to serve both science and social justice. I hope that this quest, as painful and frustrating as I have shown it to be, will entice the most idealistic and committed of this nation's youth.


### Summary Discussion

The question of reciprocity is crucial to field work. Most respondents hope to benefit from the assistance they provide to the research. Some are content with the gains of friendship. A few hope that the recording of their experiences may help others. Many informants are led by the researcher to believe his findings can serve them in their attempts to upgrade their own situations.

As a result of these expectations, the field worker will often find that his friends, informants, or respondents are ambivalent about his final report. Because of his efforts, information may become public that they have desired to keep private. Respondents may have been painted in an uncomplimentary light. The researcher's promises of reciprocity to persons and groups may have been incompletely fulfilled. Indeed, under extreme circumstances, the researcher may even be harshly condemned as an unethical and incompetent meddler by those he has studied or others who know of his work.

Social scientists have traditionally raised serious questions about these issues. Yet important dilemmas remain. Field workers are often torn between their debts to those they have studied and their commitment to a wider audience of interested colleagues, students, and readers. Researchers, particularly now, ponder how much to publish when the findings may very well enhance popular prejudices about the group studied.

This question has become acute with the recent plethora of studies on the lives of America's urban poor.

Sociologists who define themselves as radicals bristle at the "exploitation" of the less powerful.[56] They demand that their colleagues turn their attentions to and even against the influential. The rebels decry the kind of scrutinizing that exposes certain groups to the manipulation of others. Their charges are supported by the historical direction of social science research. The "problem" groups who receive a disproportionate amount of attention from researchers are often those who benefit least from the existing system. Less emphasis has been placed on studying those prestigious people whose lives and decisions often have a disastrous impact on their fellow citizens. Some social scientists now advocate putting their services at the disposal of the underprivileged.

Ability to withstand the penetrating eye of the social scientist varies markedly. High-status individuals, such as heads of administrative organizations, are often powerful and sophisticated enough to resist or manipulate social science inquiry. The great challenge to field workers remains one of penetrating into all the vital areas of social life by rejecting the temptations or threats of the influential.

I have made a crucial distinction, then, among the various types of reciprocity. Social scientists often reach understandings with respondents about the limits of their work and the protections to which informants are entitled. When these understandings concerning *personal* reciprocity are not met, social scientists may be justly accused of poor faith. In other instances, researchers adhere to the demands of *group* reciprocity and may decide to modify their own reports in order to protect the identity or legitimate interests of those they have studied. In exceptional circumstances, the investigator may actually put his materials "under lock and key" when the safety of subjects is at stake. These two components of legitimate research reciprocity are not the only instances, however, where scholarly findings are adjusted. Respondents or sponsors have also attempted to pressure investigators when research findings seem distasteful to them. *Bureaucratic* reciprocity often occurs when the social scientist is confronted by a powerful host or sponsoring agency.

Gideon Sjoberg explicitly analyzes the tension that, he feels, should exist between the social scientist and those who man the administrative control centers of modern society.[57] Social scientists, he writes, must be committed to research that exposes even the most sensitive areas of a social system. Administrators, on the other hand, are committed to maintaining the system, gathering information that will aid them in this effort, and staving off criticism that will threaten their own position. These two divergent commitments often result in conflict, as Gaylin learned.

Sjoberg cogently argues that social scientists have a great stake in defending the viability of the "private" sector in any social system. They must segregate their own role definition and role activities from the policy and administrative needs of those in decision-making positions.[58] Only in this way can they prevent themselves from becoming the "servants of power." This is an extraordinary challenge in modern urban society. Administrators, in both the public and private sector, are constantly in need of information upon which to base their decisions and are in a position to reward social scientists for their assistance. Social scientists struggling for recognition for their profession and themselves and wanting to help resolve social problems are vulnerable to pressures and the lure of economic and prestige rewards that are associated with access and service to decision-makers. Thus it is that many social scientists are accused of looking downward in the social scale for research topics and upward for research rewards.[59]

The crucial issues that Sjoberg and others have raised focus on the importance of information in adapting to complex social issues. The social scientist can always be accused of gathering data in order to enhance the influence of one group or another. Properly used, knowledge is power. The social scientist's findings certainly can be used differentially by those who have access to them and who have the means by which to implement their definitions of appropriate policy. This factor has given some social scientists reason to pause. They have asked whether field workers are unwitting accomplices of those who hope to manipulate their hosts. Field workers have responded very differently to this crucial question by maintaining the importance of knowledge in changing social policy, by advocating the need to put research skills at the service of the weak, and by becoming activists in one of the current liberation struggles. None of these approaches is without danger to the hosts or the researcher. Sjoberg has argued that social scientists must be prepared to face the wrath of important sectors of the society. Indeed, the social scientist is fulfilling his function most appropriately if no powerful group defines him as friendly to its interests.

If the social scientist is to meet the peculiar demands of his role, he must resist being co-opted by influential heads of sponsoring organizations, by groups he is studying, by university administrators intent on avoiding involvement in "hot" or controversial issues, and by his professional colleagues and organizations, who may desire to associate themselves with national or local power centers. Perhaps the major lesson comes from Becker and Dedijer, whose work I cited earlier, or from the recent statement by the uncompromising political scientist Philip Green, who also argues in support of a policy of dispersion of social science efforts.[60] No group can be allowed to monopolize the direction and utilization of research findings. Government and private bureaucracies have legitimate needs. But so do workers struggling to organize, blacks seeking to transform the system, and peace coalitions determined to resist national war policies. These groups continue to have relatively little direct access to social science.

Field workers, as men and women who have experienced the plurality of human needs and definitions and had the privilege of living among and studying others, must be acutely sensitive to the ultimate use of their efforts.[61] This will often necessitate that they self-consciously assume the stance of the outsider in their own society as they strive to serve the widest audience with their skills and findings. It is a difficult role but worth the cost for continued participation in the research adventure.[62] I am still committed and deeply attracted to that adventure.

## NOTES

1. William Foote Whyte, Appendix: "On the Evolution of Street Corner Society," *Street Corner Society* (Chicago: University of Chicago Press, 1955), particularly pp. 342–356, paperback ed.

2. Personal correspondence between William Foote Whyte and the author during December 1970.

3. Arlene Kaplan Daniels' penetrating statement deriving from her research on the military is directly appropriate to Whyte's concerns:

> The most serious ethical problem—and the one for which there is no permanent resolution—is the fact that friends in the group studied may be displeased or discomfited when research reports reach publication state. This problem is combined with the realization that, inevitably, one's own main interest in the group members is an exploitative one. Unless one moves from ceremonial to legal adoption (to become a lobbyist or "company man" in one form or another) by the group, one inevitably approaches all relationships with informants from the specialized perspective of one who eventually will withdraw. Sometimes this realization colors one's interactions to the extent that it draws reproaches from one's friends. One officer's wife, in writing a friendly letter to me, asked me if I didn't think I was too hard and too critical of the military folk. I tried to apologize for my criticism and explain how, in addition, an outsider may appear more critical than he actually is.
>
> Although I answered this wife's letter with amicability— on personal stationary rather than office letterhead—I nevertheless filed *her* friendly letter to me as part of the data under an appropriate category in my field notes. The relationship between us, and out of which the letter stemmed, illustrates the difficulties involved in the growth of friendships between the observer and the studied. ["The Low-Caste Stranger in Social Research," in Gideon Sjoberg (ed.), *Ethics, Politics and Social Research* (Cambridge, Mass.: Schenkman, 1967), p. 290].

Daniels' forthright position has apparently eased her own role conflicts. Other social scientists are far less secure in their commitment and, apparently, more receptive to the pressures of reciprocity:

> Of more serious consequence is the loyalty the researcher develops towards his hosts and informants as it may come into conflict with the primary commitment to his discipline.
>
> .     .     .
>
> This was my own principal problem in the course of writing a book on Kashmiri peasants. A good deal of very signifi-

cant information was given me by several villagers, not because I was an interested ethnographer, but because they had
come to regard me as a friend with whom they could afford
to be frank. Some of this information was vital to the adequate explanation of certain events or social changes. For
example, the first case of widow remarriage in a particular
village had taken place when a widow became pregnant and
her rich lover persuaded a man of limited means, by offering
him monetary inducement, to marry her. I must not mention
this if I ever write a book on the said village because the
villagers will see the book, and this will cause hurt feelings
as well as resentment. [T. N. Madan, "Political Pressures and
Ethical Constraints Upon Indian Sociologists" in Sjoberg
(ed.), *ibid.*, p. 174].

4. Personal correspondence between Whyte and the author during
December 1970.

5. *Ibid.*

6. It is appropriate to ask whether social science research has ever
been put to any particular use. An interesting starting point for
those pursuing this issue is Paul F. Lazarsfeld, William H. Sewell,
and Harold L. Wilensky, *The Uses of Sociology* (New York: Basic
Books, 1967). Also see Donald M. Valdes and Dwight G. Dean,
*Sociology in Use* (New York: Macmillan, 1965).

7. The entire debate is published in Arthur Vidich and Joseph Bensman, *Small Town in Mass Society* (Princeton, N.J.: Princeton University Press, 1968). The findings of the project are reported in *The
Journal of Social Issues*, 16, 4 (1960), 1-85.

8. Other social scientists have taken a strong position on the issue
of confidentiality in community studies. Lee Rainwater and David
J. Pittman argue that it is the responsibility of social scientists to
study publicly accountable behavior. Under this category they include the activities not only of public officials but also of business
men, physicians, and others, who have direct impact on broad
numbers of people. On the other hand, they maintain that it is
better to put up with the obstacles of studying these men and
women rather than to promise confidentiality when it is not
possible to provide it. See Lee Rainwater and David J. Pittman,
"Ethical Problems in Studying a Politically Sensitive and Deviant
Community," *Social Problems*, 14 (Spring 1967), 357-366.

9. A review of the history of the Princeton Center of International
Studies and a detailed listing of its financial support may be found
in, Princeton University Center of International Studies, *A Record*

of *Twenty Years 1951–1971* (Princeton, N.J.: Woodrow Wilson School of Public and International Affairs, 1971), esp. pp. 29–30. A recently completed empirical study sheds light on the reaction in Latin America to United States social scientists. See Calvin P. Blair, Richard P. Schaedel, and James H. Street, *Responsibilities of the Foreign Scholar to the Local Scholarly Community: Studies of U.S. Research in Guatemala, Chile and Paraguay.* (Published jointly by the Council on Educational Cooperation with Latin America, Education and World Affairs and the Latin American Studies Association, 1969). It surveys social science research in these countries during the 1950s and 1960s.

10. Personal correspondence between Gerald D. Berreman and the author dated March 3, 1971.

11. Gerald D. Berreman, *Hindus of the Himalayas,* 2d ed. (Berkeley: University of California Press, 1972).

12. For further discussion of the issue of research sponsorship, see Ralph L. Beals, *Politics of Social Research* (Chicago: Aldine, 1968), particularly Chapter 4, which talks about "The Use and Support of Social Research." Also see "Social Science and the Federal Government," *The Annals,* 394 (March 1971). The entire issue of the journal is devoted to a variety of topics pertinent to our discussion.

13. *The New York Times,* August 14, 1968.

14. Similar types of problems face scholars working on the affairs of the communist world. It is quite common to hear them discuss their reluctance to publish certain kinds of material particularly about the Soviet Union. They know that it is possible that the writing of critical statements may preclude their receiving an entrance visa in the future. Conversely, one scholar recently refused to sign an open letter advocating the admission of Mainland China to the United Nations. He felt that such an endorsement might lead the Nationalist Chinese authorities to reject his application for further study in their country. Moreover, he felt a keen sense of loyalty to the many Chinese on Taiwan who had assisted him in his work. The "China question" was of great concern to them and he felt that his signing the petition would be interpreted by them as a stab in the back.

15. The issues of reciprocity involved in the selection of a research problem and the impact of the findings on hosts is further compounded by the serious charge of "research colonialism." Many Latin Americans have contended that, in spite of all protestations, most United States academics are more concerned with advancing their careers than in contributing to the welfare of the people

being studied. Kalman Silvert, a distinguished political scientist with long years of experience in Latin America, is in basic agreement with this view, and he has bitterly condemned those American investigators who are more interested in securing the benefits of their work for themselves, their departments, and their universities. Kalman Silvert, "American Academic Ethics and Social Science Abroad: The Lesson of Project Camelot" in Irving Louis Horowitz (ed.), *The Rise and Fall of Project Camelot* (Cambridge, Mass.: M.I.T. Press, 1967), pp. 80–106.

Johan Galtung, who is deeply committed to developing social science in Latin America, has specifically focused his attention on this increasingly complex issue. Scholars, he has urged, should be dedicated to training those who are associated with their projects in the host country. This training should go far beyond the teaching of interviewing skills. Local personnel should be involved with the design of the study, its execution, and the analysis of the data. In short, they should be fully incorporated into the research process. This effort can help reestablish confidence in the integrity and good will of United States social scientists and vitiate accusations that we are "imperialists" determined to "mine" data without consideration for the well-being of local populations. Johan Galtung, "After Camelot" in Horowitz (ed.), *op. cit.*, pp. 281–312.

16. For a stinging critique by a young United States scholar, see Philip G. Altbach, "Education and Neocolonialism," *Teachers College Record*, 72 (May 1971), 544–558.

17. For an insightful account by an Indian scholar on some of the problems of studying his own society, see M. N. Srinivas, *Social Change in Modern India* (Berkeley: University of California Press, 1967).

18. Gerald D. Berreman's latest thoughts were presented at the 15th Annual Meeting of the Kroeber Anthropological Society (May 9, 1971) under the title "Bringing It All Back Home."

19. Delmos J. Jones, "Social Responsibility and the Belief in Basic Research: An Example from Thailand," *Current Anthropology*, 12 (June 1971), 347–350.

20. *The New York Times*, January 13, 1970.

21. To give you some further insight into this I enclose a *xerox* of the concluding chapter to the project final report. The "hard-nosed" quality of the writing was partly deliberate in an attempt to reach a military audience, but it also, more than I like to admit today, reflects my own attitudes at the time of writing. Refugees offered us a "pacification resource"

and our error was in not fully "exploiting" that resource. The conclusions aren't wrong—in my rather biased opinion, the chapter represents one of the more coherent available analyses of the employment of human resources in revolutionary warfare—and the government policy makers got the answers to a lot of rather important questions (not that any of our findings or recommendations were ever taken into account when policy was made—but that's a whole other issue) but there is a callous quality to it all which I now find disturbing. But again, I worked in Vietnam as a committed participant in the war and my intent in all of my work was to conduct research that would help the Allies to win. To this end I took my interviewers into insecure areas where no uncommitted social scientist purely interested in the pursuit of knowledge would ever voluntarily go. I personally accompanied Vietnamese army combat patrols, on which I wore a camouflage suit and carried a weapon (and suffered considerable fear in the process), and by the end of the field study had driven myself close to the point of complete mental and physical exhaustion. Except for the final point which I seem to be skillfully replicating while writing my dissertation, I would certainly *not* engage in such activities in the interests of advancing either science or my own career.

Personal correspondence between A. Terry Rambo and the author dated January 8, 1971.

22. And I must admit that I had a desire for adventure—the war was not only moral, it was exciting. Maybe it wasn't quite the China of Malraux or Hemingway's Spain, but one could still carry a submachine gun around—maybe even have to use it—while intriguing with the various local "warlords" composing the Vietnamese and American official establishments. It was a huge game that I played well and very much enjoyed until one afternoon I had to drive a jeep down a road that I knew might be mined—an incident, if I may parody your style, in which Terry Rambo, boy operations researcher, discovers what nausea is all about and loses all further interest in the glamour of guerrilla warfare.

Personal correspondence between A. Terry Rambo and the author dated January 8, 1971.

23. Personal correspondence between A. Terry Rambo and the author dated January 23, 1971.

**24.** Pierre L. van den Berghe, whose research on South Africa was discussed earlier ("Research in South Africa: The Story of My Experiences with Tyranny," in Sjoberg (ed.), *op. cit.*, pp. 183–197.), continues to ponder about the impact of a subsequent field work experience:

> The kind of ethical problems I face in connection with my most recent field work in Nigeria are, if anything, even more agonizing than those I encountered in South Africa where I had no ambivalence about the system I was studying. In Nigeria, I studied power, class, and ethnicity at the university where I had been invited as a Visiting Professor by the local sociology department.

.   .   .

> The problem is simply that my study will be one continuous indictment of the university as an exotic, ill-adapted, wasteful, elitist institution whose prime function is to create and perpetuate the mandarinate which rules the country for its nearly exclusive benefit. In fact, my study will, I believe, be the first documented case study of the predatory and exploitative character of what Fanon somewhat misleadingly called the "national bourgeoisie." From a draft of one chapter on ethnic conflicts, it is clear that most academics, both expatriates and Nigerians, are quite irate at me, all the more so as they will find it very difficult to attack my integrity. The best they will be able to do is to try to brand me as a racist, but I doubt that they will be successful.

> What I find so traumatic about the whole thing is that, as a member of the mandarinate I attack, I feel very ambivalent toward the culture it represents. All my strictures are completely honest, but, at the same time, I found the intellectual and cultural climate exhilarating in the extreme. I simply thrived in that high-quality intellectual environment, took delight in my bright and highly motivated students, savored the political sophistication and urbane cynicism of my colleagues, and soaked in the stimulating artistic culture. And needless to say, I established very friendly relations with many people whom I collectively attack as a class.

Personal correspondence between Pierre L. van den Berghe and the author dated November 24, 1970.

**25.** For a summary of the factors involved in this changing definition, see Robert H. Bohlke, "The Activist, Value-Committed Sociologist:

An Emerging Role." Paper presented at the 38th Annual Meeting of the Eastern Sociological Society, Boston, Massachusetts, April 6, 1968. Bohlke is in the Department of Sociology, American International College, Springfield, Massachusetts.

26. Rainwater and Pittman, *op. cit.*

27. *Ibid.*, p. 361.

28. Martin Nicolaus, "The A.S.A. Convention," *Catalyst* (Spring 1969), p. 105.

29. Oscar Lewis' conception of the culture of poverty is discussed in his introduction to his book on Puerto Rican life on the island and in New York City, *La Vida* (New York: Random House, 1968).

30. For an important critique of Oscar Lewis, see Charles Valentine, *Culture and Poverty* (Chicago: University of Chicago Press, 1968). For a sophisticated study that is also critical of the Lewis approach, see Murray Gruber, "The Non-Culture of Poverty: Aspirations, Expectations and Militancy Among Black Youth," unpublished paper. Gruber is currently on the faculty of the School for Applied Social Sciences, Case-Western Reserve University, Cleveland, Ohio.

31. Elliot Liebow, *Tally's Corner* (Boston: Little, Brown, 1967). Liebow elaborated his position in several lengthy telephone conversations with the author during the winter, spring, and fall of 1971.

32. Some of the most important accounts of the black urban experience have been written by black researchers. See Kenneth B. Clark, *Dark Ghetto* (New York: Harper & Row, 1965); and William Moore, Jr., *The Vertical Ghetto* (New York: Random House, 1969). Both of these men, and many like them, are committed social scientists who believe that research and writing can make an important contribution to understanding and uplifting black and other oppressed peoples in this society and elsewhere.

33. Bernard Farber, David L. Harvey, and Michael Lewis, *Community, Kinship, and Competence*, Research and Development Program on Preschool Disadvantaged Children (Washington, D.C.: U.S. Department of Health, Education, and Welfare, 1969), Vol. III. Michael Lewis and the author have had many conversations during the last two years that have explored the development of Lewis' thinking and research.

34. Michael Lewis has also turned his attention very sharply to the gains that accrue to whites because of the limitation on opportunity for blacks and other minority groups. In an incisive critique he indicates that black liberation will not occur until whites hon-

estly confront the social benefits of oppression. Michael Lewis, "Social Inequality and Social Problems," in Jack D. Douglas (ed.), *American Social Problems in a Revolutionary Age* (New York: Random House, forthcoming.)

35. Marc Pilisuk, "People's Park, Power and the Calling of the Social Sciences," in Robert Buckhaut, *et al.* (eds.), *Toward Social Change: A Handbook for Those Who Would* (New York: Harper & Row, 1971.)

36. Henry A. Landsberger, "Southern Rural Cooperatives: A Provocative Preliminary Assessment of Their Past and Their Prospects," unpublished paper, pp. 11–12. Landsberger is in the Department of Sociology, University of North Carolina, Chapel Hill, North Carolina.

37. Howard S. Becker and Steven Dedijer, *Counter-Establishment R & D*, unpublished paper. Becker is in the Department of Sociology, Northwestern University, Evanston, Illinois.

38. An excellent source for those concerned with radical scholars and scholarship is the New England Free Press, 791 Tremont Street, Boston, Massachusetts 02118. The press produces a wide variety of pamphlet material on such issues as Latin America, racism, the working class, early socialization, Women's Liberation, ecology, and the economy. For example, one of its recent pamphlets is written by G. William Domhoff, author of *Who Rules America?* (Englewood Cliffs, N.J.: Prentice-Hall, 1967); and *The Higher Circles: The Governing Class of America* (New York: Random House, 1970). Domhoff's pamphlet, *Researching the Governing Class of America*, is extremely useful for those interested in readily available material on the political and financial elite in this country. Domhoff states, "The single most valuable source in all types of 'power structure' research is *Who's Who in America*, which contains a great deal of information on most of the people it lists." Domhoff cites other sources such as the various *Who's Who* in different geographical sectors of the country and within different ethnic groups. Domhoff also lists appropriate reference material for those concerned with businessmen and financiers, lawyers, political leaders and government officials, and foundation officers and trustees.

Another fascinating source for unusual ideas, research projects, and bibliography is *The Subterranean Sociology Newsletter*, edited by the talented Marcello Truzzi, a member of the Department of Sociology at New College in Florida. The newsletter is available simply for the asking. The December 1971 issue, for example, contains a listing of Radical Sociology Periodicals.

39. Other social scientists advocate a third-force position between the

"old" sociology and the radical activists. The middle position would recruit men and women deeply concerned about the solution of major social problems, but wary of the pitfalls of commitment to particular movements. Funds would be collected among social scientists and private foundations to support research and action projects. Robert H. Bohlke "Thoughts on the 'Prostitution' of Sociologists." Paper presented at the 65th Annual Meeting of the American Sociological Association, August, 1970.

40. Laud Humphreys, *Tearoom Trade* (Chicago: Aldine, 1970); "Tearoom Trade: Impersonal Sex in Public Places," *Transaction* (January 1970), pp. 10–26.

41. Personal correspondence between Laud Humphreys and the author dated February 24, 1971.

42. *Ibid.*

43. *Ibid.*

44. For a pungent article recounting the issue read Tom Wicker, "The Goat and the Cabbage Patch," *The New York Times*, March 11, 1971, p. 39.

45. Personal correspondence between Humphreys and the author dated February 24, 1971.

46. The controversy can have highly positive consequences. It can also result in irreconcilable cleavages among sociologists. This last position is cogently argued by Robert H. Bohlke, "The Nature and Consequences of the Coming 'War' Between Sociologists," unpublished paper written in December 1968.

47. Howard S. Becker and Raymond W. Mack make some astute observations on the problems of switching gears:

Today, few sociologists have the temerity to be square, resist fashionable radicalism, and associate with businessmen So today, paradoxically, we may assign high priority to the study of the "ruling circles," the higher and highest levels of government, business, and the military, a priority dictated by radical life styles. But those same radical life styles cut off for many sociologists all but the most formal, public, and difficult avenues of access to such materials. Only someone who has cultivated those avenues of entry for years, by paying the dues of living in the style that would make him *persona grata* to the right people, will be in a position to do that research. Howard S. Becker and Raymond W. Mack, "Unobtrusive Entry and Accidental Access to Field Data," unpublished paper prepared for a conference on "Methodological Problems in Comparative Sociological Research" held at the Institute for Comparative Sociology, Indiana University, Bloomington, Indiana, April 8–9, 1971, p. 10. Both authors are on the faculty of Northwestern University, Evanston, Illinois.

48. Jane Cassels Record, "The Research Institute and the Pressure Group," in Sjoberg (ed.), *op. cit.*, pp. 25–49.

49. Simon Marcson, *The Scientist in American Industry* (Princeton, N.J.: Industrial Relations Section, Princeton University, 1960).

50. Renée C. Fox similarly encountered a wide variety of response to her critical analysis of Belgian medical research. Some physicians applauded her work while others characterized her as an ignorant, meddling foreigner. She was asked to speak to a wide variety of groups in Belgium and also found herself continually approached by practitioners who provided her with their own stories, which corroborated her analyses. Many of these people seemed to feel that they would be strengthened if their situations were put before her. It was quite obvious that her research had become a crucial weapon in the struggle to reform the Belgian medical establishment. Renée C. Fox, "An American Sociologist in the Land of Belgian Medical Practice," in Phillip E. Hammond (ed.), *Sociologists at Work* (Garden City, N.Y.: Anchor Books, 1968), pp. 399–452.

51. Daniels, *op cit.*, p. 289.

52. Willard Gaylin, *In The Service of Their Country/War Resisters in Prison* (New York: Viking, 1970).

53. Personal correspondence between Willard Gaylin and the author during spring and summer 1971.

54. *Ibid.*

55. *Ibid.*

56. There are many articles and books dealing with radical thinking in American social science. For several useful recent collections, see Stephen E. Deutsch and John Howard (eds.), *Where It's At: Radical Perspectives in Sociology* (New York: Harper & Row, 1970); David Colfax and Jack Roach (eds.), *Radical Sociology* (New York: Basic Books, 1971); and the entire issue of *Sociological Inquiry*, 40 (Winter 1970).

57. Gideo Sjoberg, "Project Camelot: Selected Reactions and Personal Reflections" in Sjoberg (ed.), *op. cit.*, pp. 141–161.

58. For an elaboration of his views, see Gideon Sjoberg and Roger

Nepp, *A Methodology for Social Research* (New York: Harper & Row, 1968), esp. Chapter 4.

59. Nicolaus, *op. cit.*, pp. 103–106.

60. Philip Green, "The Obligations of American Social Scientists," *The Annals*, 394 (March 1971), 13–27.

61. For a positive statement about the possibilities of this effort, see Ely Chinoy, *Knowledge and Action: The Role of Sociology* (Northampton, Mass.: Smith College, 1970).

62. Two excellent collections of essays serve as continual reference points for the self-critical sociologist. Maurice Stein and Arthur Vidich (eds.), *Sociology on Trial* (Englewood Cliffs, N.J.: Prentice-Hall, 1963); and Irving Louis Horowitz (ed.), *The New Sociology* (New York: Oxford University Press, 1964).

# BIBLIOGRAPHY

Those interested in pursuing their study of the research adventure should note that there are now available a significant number of edited volumes that have collected a rich array of field work experiences. These are indicated by an asterisk.

*ADAMS, RICHARD N., and JACK J. PREISS (eds.). *Human Organization Research.* Homewood, Ill.: Dorsey Press, 1960.

ALTBACH, PHILIP G. "Education and Neocolonialism," *Teachers College Record,* 72, May 1971, 544–558.

BEALS, RALPH L. *Politics of Social Research.* Chicago: Aldine, 1968.

BECKER, HOWARD S., and STEVEN DEDIJER. *Counter-Establishment R & D.* Unpublished paper.

BECKER, HOWARD S., BLANCHE GEER, DAVID RIESMAN, ROBERT S. WEISS (eds.). *Institutions and the Person.* Chicago: Aldine, 1968.

BECKER, HOWARD S., and RAYMOND W. MACK. "Unobtrusive Entry and Accidental Access to Field Data." Unpublished paper prepared for a conference on "Methodological Problems in Comparative Sociological Research" held at the Institute for Comparative Sociology, Indiana University, Bloomington, Indiana, April 8–9, 1971.

BELL, DANIEL. "Crime As An American Way of Life," in his *The End of Ideology.* New York: Free Press, 1960.

BERGER, PETER L. *Invitation to Sociology: A Humanistic Perspective.* New York: Anchor Books, 1963.

BERREMAN, GERALD D. *Behind Many Masks.* Ithaca: The Society for Applied Anthropology, 1962.

————. *Hindus of the Himalayas.* Berkeley: University of California Press, 1963.

*BICKMAN, LEONARD, and THOMAS HENCHY (eds.). *Beyond the Laboratory: Field Research in Social Psychology.* New York: McGraw-Hill, 1972.

BLAIR, CALVIN P., RICHARD P. SCHAEDEL, and JAMES H. STREET. *Responsibilities of the Foreign Scholar to the Local Scholarly Community: Studies of U.S. Research in Guatemala, Chile and Paraguay.* The Council on Educational Cooperation with Latin America, Education and World Affairs and the Latin American Studies Association, 1969.

BOGUSLAW, ROBERT. "Ethics and the Social Scientist," in I. L. Horowitz (ed.), *The Rise and Fall of Project Camelot.* Cambridge: M.I.T. Press, 1967.

BOHLKE, ROBERT H. "The Activist, Value-Committed Sociologist: An Emerging Role." Paper presented at the 38th Annual Meeting of the Eastern Sociological Society, Boston, Massachusetts, April 6, 1968.

————. "The Nature and Consequences of the Coming 'War' Between Sociologists." Unpublished paper written in December 1968.

————. "Thoughts on the 'Prostitution' of Sociologists." Paper presented at the 65th Annual Meeting of the American Sociological Association, August 1970.

BONILLA, FRANK, and MYRON GLAZER. Appendix A: "A Note on Methodology. Field Work in a Hostile Environment: A Chapter in the Sociology of Social Research in Chile," *Student Politics in Chile.* New York: Basic Books, 1970.

BOWEN, ELENORE SMITH. *Return to Laughter.* New York: Harper & Row, 1954.

CHINOY, ELY. *Knowledge and Action: The Role of Sociology.* Northampton, Mass.: Smith College, 1970.

CLARK, KENNETH B. *Dark Ghetto.* New York: Harper & Row, 1965.

COLFAX, DAVID J. "Pressure Toward Distortion and Involvement in Studying a Civil Rights Organization," *Human Organization,* 25, Summer 1966, 140–149.

*————. and JACK ROACH (eds.). *Radical Sociology.* New York: Basic Books, 1971.

DANIELS, ARLENE KAPLAN. "The Low-Caste Stranger in Social Research," in Gideon Sjoberg (ed.), *Ethics, Politics and Social Research.* Cambridge: Schenkman, 1967.

DENZIN, NORMAN K. *The Research Act; A Theoretical Introduction to Sociological Methods.* Chicago: Aldine, 1970.

——. (ed.). *The Values of Social Science.* Chicago: Aldine, 1970.

DE SOLA POOL, ITHIEL. "The Necessity for Social Scientists Doing Research for Government," in I. L. Horowitz (ed.), *The Rise and Fall of Project Camelot.* Cambridge: M.I.T. Press, 1967.

*DEUTSCH, STEPHEN E., and JOHN HOWARD (eds.), *Where It's At: Radical Perspectives in Sociology.* New York: Harper & Row, 1970.

*DOUGLAS, JACK D. (ed.). *Observations of Deviance.* New York: Random House, 1970.

FARBER, BERNARD, DAVID L. HARVEY, and MICHAEL LEWIS. "Community, Kinship, and Competence," *Research and Development Program on Preschool Disadvantaged Children,* Vol. III. Washington, D.C.: U.S. Department of Health, Education, and Welfare, 1969.

FOX, RENÉE C. "An American Sociologist in the Land of Belgian Medical Research," in Phillip E. Hammond (ed.), *Sociologists at Work.* New York: Anchor Books, 1968.

*FREILICH, MORRIS (ed.). *Marginal Natives: Anthropologists at Work.* New York: Harper & Row, 1970.

GALTUNG, JOHAN. "After Camelot," in I. L. Horowitz (ed.), *The Rise and Fall of Project Camelot.* Cambridge: M.I.T. Press, 1967.

GANS, HERBERT J. *The Levittowners.* New York: Pantheon Books, 1967.

——. "The Participant-Observer as a Human Being: Observations on the Personal Aspects of Field Work," in Howard S. Becker, *et al.* (eds.), *Institutions and the Person.* Chicago: Aldine, 1968.

GAYLIN, WILLARD. *In the Service of Their Country/War Resisters in Prison.* New York: Viking, 1970.

GEER, BLANCHE. "First Days in the Field," in Phillip E. Hammond (ed.), *Sociologists at Work.* New York: Anchor Books, 1968.

GLASER, BARNEY G., and ANSELM L. STRAUSS. *The Discovery of Grounded Theory.* Chicago: Aldine, 1967.

GOFFMAN, ERVING. *The Presentation of Self in Everyday Life.* New York: Anchor Books, 1959.

*GOLDE, PEGGY (ed.). *Women in the Field.* Chicago: Aldine, 1970.

GOODE, WILLIAM. "Communications to the Editor," *American Sociologist,* I, November 1966, 255–257.

GREEN, PHILIP. "The Obligations of American Social Scientists," *The Annals*, 394, March 1971, 13–27.

GRUBER, MURRAY. "The Non-Culture of Poverty: Aspirations, Expectations and Militancy Among Black Youth." Unpublished Paper.

*HABENSTEIN, ROBERT W. (ed.). *Pathways to Data*. Chicago: Aldine, 1970.

*HAMMOND, PHILLIP E. *Sociologists at Work*. New York: Anchor Books, 1968.

HANNERZ, ULF. *Soulside: Inquiries into Ghetto Culture and Community*. New York: Columbia University Press, 1969.

*HENRY, FRANCES, and SATISH SABERWAL (eds.). *Stress and Response in Field Work*. New York: Holt, Rinehart & Winston, 1969.

HOROWITZ, IRVING LOUIS (ed.). *The New Sociology*. New York: Oxford University Press, 1964.

———. "The Rise and Fall of Project Camelot," in I. L. Horowitz (ed.), *The Rise and Fall of Project Camelot*. Cambridge: M.I.T. Press, 1967.

HUMPHREYS, LAUD. *Tearoom Trade*. Chicago: Aldine, 1970.

———. "Tearoom Trade: Impersonal Sex in Public Places," *Transaction*, January 1970, pp. 10–26.

*JACOBS, GLENN (ed.). *The Participant Observer*. New York: Braziller, 1970.

JONES, DELMOS J. "Social Responsibility and the Belief in Basic Research: An Example from Thailand," *Current Anthropology*, 12, June 1971, 347–350.

JUNKER, BUFORD H. *Field Work*. Chicago: University of Chicago Press, 1960.

KELMAN, HERBERT C. *A Time to Speak: On Human Values and Social Research*. San Francisco: Jossey-Bass, 1968.

LAZARSFELD, PAUL F., WILLIAM H. SEWELL, and HAROLD L. WILENSKY. *The Uses of Sociology*. New York: Basic Books, 1967.

LEWIS, MICHAEL. "Social Inequality and Social Problems," in Jack D. Douglas (ed.), *American Social Problems in a Revolutionary Age*. New York: Random House, forthcoming.

LEWIS, OSCAR. *La Vida*. New York: Random House, 1968.

LIEBOW, ELLIOT. *Tally's Corner*. Boston: Little, Brown, 1967.

LURIE, ALISON. *Imaginary Friends*. New York: Coward-McCann, 1967.

MADAN, T. N. "Political Pressures and Ethical Constraints Upon

Indian Sociologists," in Gideon Sjoberg (ed.), *Ethics, Politics and Social Research*. Cambridge: Schenkman, 1967.

MADGE, JOHN. *The Origins of Scientific Sociology*. New York: Free Press, 1962.

MARCSON, SIMON. *The Scientist in American Industry*. Princeton, N.J.: Industrial Relations Section, Princeton University, 1960.

*MCCALL, GEORGE J. and J. L. SIMMONS (eds.). *Issues in Participant Observations: A Text and Reader*. Reading, Mass.: Addison-Wesley, 1969.

MERTON, ROBERT K. "Manifest and Latent Functions," in his *Social Theory and Social Structure*. New York: Free Press, 1957.

MOORE, WILLIAM, JR. *The Vertical Ghetto*. New York: Random House, 1969.

NASH, DENNISON. "The Ethnologist as Stranger: An Essay in the Sociology of Knowledge," *Southwestern Journal of Anthropology*, 19, Summer 1963, 149–167.

NICOLAUS, MARTIN. "The A.S.A. Convention," *Catalyst*, Spring 1969, pp. 103–106.

PHILLIPS, DEREK L. *Knowledge from What?* Chicago: Rand McNally, 1971.

*PILISUK, MARC. "People's Park, Power and the Calling of the Social Sciences," in Robert Buckhaut, *et al*. (eds.), *Toward Social Change: A Handbook for Those Who Would*. New York: Harper & Row, 1971.

RAINWATER, LEE, and DAVID J. PITTMAN. "Ethical Problems in Studying a Politically Sensitive and Deviant Community," *Social Problems*, 14, Spring 1967, 357–366.

RECORD, JANE CASSELS. "The Research Institute and the Pressure Group," in Gideon Sjoberg (ed.), *Ethics, Politics and Social Research*. Cambridge: Schenkman, 1967.

*Recording of Jury Deliberations*. Hearings Before the Subcommittee to Investigate the Administration of the Internal Security Act and Other Internal Security Laws of the Committee on the Judiciary, United States Senate, Eighty-Fourth Congress, First Session, October 12 and 13, 1955. Washington, D.C.: Government Printing Office, 1955.

*REYNOLDS, LARRY T., and JANICE M. REYNOLDS (eds.). *The Sociology of Sociology*. New York: David McKay, 1970.

SAHLINS, MARSHALL. "The Established Order: Do Not Fold, Spindle, or Mutilate," in I. L. Horowitz (ed.), *The Rise and Fall of Project Camelot*. Cambridge: M.I.T. Press, 1967.

*SHOSTAK, ARTHUR B. (ed.). *Sociology in Action*. Homewood, Ill.: Dorsey, 1966.

SILVERT, KALMAN H. "American Academic Ethics and Social Science Abroad: The Lesson of Project Camlot," in I. L. Horowitz (ed.), *The Rise and Fall of Project Camelot*. Cambridge: M.I.T. Press, 1967.

SIMON, JULIAN L. *Basic Research Methods in Social Science*. New York: Random House, 1969.

SJOBERG, GIDEON, and ROGER NEPP. *A Methodology for Social Research*. New York: Harper & Row, 1968.

*SJOBERG, GIDEON (ed.). *Ethics, Politics and Social Research*. Cambridge: Schenkman, 1967.

———. "Project Camelot: Selected Reactions and Personal Reflections," in Gideon Sjoberg (ed.), *Ethics, Politics and Social Research*. Cambridge: Schenkman, 1967.

*Sociological Inquiry*, Vol. 40, Winter, 1970.

SRINIVAS, M. N. *Social Change in Modern India*. Berkeley: University of California Press, 1967.

STEIN, MAURICE, and ARTHUR VIDICH (eds.). *Sociology on Trial*. Englewood Cliffs, N.J.: Prentice-Hall, 1963.

*VALDES, DONALD M., and DWIGHT G. DEAN. *Sociology in Use*. New York: Macmillan, 1965.

VALENTINE, CHARLES. *Culture and Poverty*. Chicago: University of Chicago Press, 1968.

VAN DEN BERGHE, PIERRE L. *Caneville: The Social Structure of a South African Town*. Middletown, Conn.: Wesleyan University Press, 1964.

———. *Race and Racism*. New York: John Wiley, 1967.

———. "Research in South Africa: The Story of My Experiences with Tyranny," in Gideon Sjoberg (ed.), *Ethics, Politics and Social Research*. Cambridge: Schenkman, 1967.

———. *South Africa*. Middletown, Conn.: Wesleyan University Press, 1965.

VAUGHAN, TED R. "Governmental Intervention in Social Research: Political and Ethical Dimensions in the Wichita Jury Records," in Gideon Sjoberg (ed.), *Ethics, Politics and Social Research*. Cambridge: Schenkman, 1967.

VIDICH, ARTHUR, and JOSEPH BENSMAN. *Small Town in Mass Society*. Princeton, N.J.: Princeton University Press, 1968.

———, MAURICE R. STEIN. *Reflections on Community Studies*. New York: John Wiley, 1964.

VON HOFFFMAN, NICHOLAS, IRVING LOUIS HOROWITZ, and LEE RAIN-WATER. "Sociological Snoopers and Journalistic Moralizers: An Exchange," *Transaction*, May 1970, pp. 4–8.

*WARD, ROBERT E., *et al. Studying Politics Abroad*. Boston: Little, Brown, 1964.

*WEBB, E. J., D. T. CAMPBELL, R. D. SCHWARTZ, and L. SECHREST. *Unobtrusive Measures: Nonreactive Research in the Social Sciences*. Chicago: Rand McNally, 1966.

WHYTE, WILLIAM FOOTE. "The Role of the U.S. Professor in Developing Countries," *American Sociologist*. 4, February 1969, 19–28.

———. *Street Corner Society*. Chicago: University of Chicago Press, 1955.

WICKER, TOM. "The Goat and the Cabbage Patch." *The New York Times*, March 11, 1971.

# NAME INDEX